"Only Thirty Birthdays"

Tees Towing's COALOPOLIS (built 1923) towing the three-masted ship GARTHNEILL (built 1885) to sea. Both vessels were entered in British Marine. (J.H. Proud)

"Only Thirty Birthdays"

British Marine Mutual, 1876 to 1996

L. J. Paterson, B.Sc., Ph.D., F.R.S.A.

By the same author: Twelve Hundred Miles for Thirty Shillings

© L.J. Paterson, 1996

ISBN: 0-9528152-0-6 cloth bound edition.
0-9528152-1-4 leather bound edition.

Published by: The British Marine Mutual Insurance Association Ltd.,
Walsingham House, 35, Seething Lane, London EC3N 4DQ.

Design consultants: Buffey & Buffey, 6, Queen Street,
Coggeshall, Essex CO6 1UF.

Typeset and Repro by: Klip Graphics, Unit 19, Fairground Way,
Walsall, West Midlands WS1 4NU

Printed by: William Gibbons & Sons Ltd.,
Wolverhampton, West Midlands WV13 3XT.

Contents

The DUKE OF EDINBURGH, a wooden hulled sailing ship of 1118 g.r.t. built in 1867, was the first entry to the newly incorporated Association in 1876.

BUCKINGHAM PALACE.

It is a remarkable coincidence that the first ship to be insured by British Marine after its incorporation 120 years ago was a three-masted ship owned by Foley and Company of Fenchurch Street and named 'Duke of Edinburgh'. The Duke of Edinburgh at the time was my great grand uncle who enjoyed a long and successful career in the Royal Navy.

I congratulate British Marine on its record of writing insurance for the British Merchant Navy over the last 120 years. I hope it will prosper for many years to come.

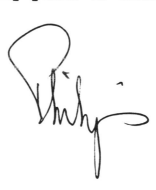

A forward from His Royal Highness, Prince Philip, the Duke of Edinburgh.

Acknowledgements

I would like to acknowledge the support that I have had from many people in the production of this book.

To Richard Leslie (whose idea it was to have an up-dated history for the thirtieth birthday) and all of the staff at British Marine, past and present, for help with the gathering of information and photographs, I am grateful. Of the staff, Bruce Fenwick played a special role in providing information from the Evans family archives. Bill Devlin and Tony Winter, both former directors, helped with information and photographs and they and all the other members of the Association who gave permission to have photographs of their vessels reproduced are also due our thanks. Frau Ingrid Clausius was very helpful in providing information on the early days of the growth of the Association in Germany.

David Burrell, of the World Ship Society, gave invaluable assistance in the practical matter of guiding the publication through the printing processes (he also provided data on some of the ships) and Sue Buffey's contribution to the design of the book in the British Marine 'house style' was much appreciated.

Finally, tribute is due to Christine Pratt without whose meticulous researching of the British Marine records this book could not have been produced on time and with the quality of information that it contains. Her suggestions on background information were helpful and intelligent and she undertook all of her tasks, including those that led to dead ends, with patience and good humour.

Preface

February has always been an important month for British Marine Mutual. Traditionally the insurance year began on the 20th of February, the date when the Baltic Sea would be likely to be free of ice and a new season's trade could begin.

February was also the month in which British Marine was incorporated as a limited liability company and registered at Company House. For the cost of just twenty pounds Mr. E.C. Curzon, the Registrar of Joint Stock Companies, issued a certificate inscribed "Given under my hand at London this twenty-ninth day of February One Thousand Eight Hundred and Seventy-Six". What better year for the great leap forward than one divisible by four? But if British Marine has a birthday once in four years, just how old is it? Is it one hundred and twenty or only thirty years?

Either would seem to be a slightly odd anniversary to celebrate in any special way. Organisations, like people, commemorate silver jubilees and centenaries, but thirty or one hundred and twenty? So why the effort now? Anthony Brown's 1976 booklet, a model of elegant and informative writing, is now over twenty years old and describes an Association that is hardly recognisable today. The changes in the shipping and insurance markets, to which the Association has responded, have been significant. The time is ripe therefore to set down the record of the last two decades and take a considered backward look before moving on again. Hence this new book.

Our predecessors were quite clear that British Marine really set up shop in 1866. The members of the day certainly held a centenary dinner, in 1966, in Trinity House, round the corner from our present offices at Seething Lane, to celebrate the event as they saw it. And they did so with some justification as there is a certain amount of evidence that indicated that the British Marine Club was in operation under the management of E.R. Evans, in the 1860's.

So how old is British Marine in 1996? One hundred and twenty, or one hundred and thirty or perhaps a little more? On the whole it seems much safer to count the leap years and claim only thirty birthdays.

No. 10383 C

N.L. 10001

Certificate of Incorporation

OF THE

British Marine Mutual Insurance Association Limited

I hereby Certify, That the

British Marine Mutual Insurance Association Limited

is this day Incorporated under the Companies Act, 1862, and that this Company is **Limited**.

Given under my hand at London, this *twenty ninth* day of *February* One Thousand Eight Hundred and Seventy *Six*

Fee: £20.

E G Cusson

Registrar of Joint Stock Companies.

s. 18.

The Certificate of Incorporation, dated 29th of February 1876.

In the Beginning

The origins of the mutual writing of marine insurances are lost in the mists of time but evidence of association for communal protection exists in the ancient civilisations of China, India and Phoenicia. The Greeks and Romans had organisations which provided mutual protection for illness and burial expenses. The craft guilds of medieval Europe had, as a subsidiary activity to the preservation of skills and the promotion of goods, the self-help of their members against the trials and tribulations of a very harsh life.

In a more modern European context Italian traders from the city state of Genoa are known to have had marine insurance policies in place in the late 13th century. Shakespeare may have had the Merchant of Venice uncovered against loss when he wrote in 1596. (There would be no story to tell had Antonio been able to discharge his debts.) That may have been artistic license rather than reflection of the practice in the London of those days. Of course then, as today, owners could choose to be self-insured. These Italian policies set a form and standard for use in England and elsewhere as they are referred to in legal disputes in the High Court of Admiralty in the mid-16th century. The same records tell us that there were 'sworn brokers' (they swore to uphold good practices and to keep accurate records of their transactions) in the City of London who wrote marine insurance. A Chamber of Assurances was established in 1576 and was certainly still in existence over a century later.

Around this time Edward Lloyd's coffee house became a popular venue for those offering insurance and while it is not the purpose of this book to repeat that well-known story, we note that the name became used and associated with a body of subscribers, some 150 in number, in the early 18th century which generally set insurance rates that were widely followed throughout the rest of Britain. There were markets in provincial ports like Newcastle, Bristol and Glasgow. But, for example, the Glasgow 'Tobacco Lords', who traded extensively with Virginia and West Indies, found that the local underwriters followed closely where Lloyd's led.

Nevertheless these provincial markets grew in strength and confidence as the century passed and provided the nucleus for independent action when the need and desire arose. The 18th century also saw the growth of the 'Friendly Societies', truly mutual organisations, for the protection of members of society in general against the misfortunes of life. Against this social background the extension of the concept to trade and to shipping was natural and inevitable, particularly as problems arose with the established forms of marine insurance towards the end of the century.

In 1720, two companies, Royal Exchange Assurance and London Assurance, received Royal Charters for transacting marine insurance and legally the market for the writing of policies for marine risk became restricted to these companies and to Lloyd's. This stabilised the situation after a period of wild speculative activity and both the corporate and the private underwriters prospered for a time.

Articles of Association

OF

THE BRITISH MARINE MUTUAL.

INSURANCE ASSOCIATION, LIMITED.

INTERPRETATION.

1. In the interpretation of these presents, the following words and expressions shall have the following meanings, unless such meanings be inconsistent with the subject or context, that is to say:—

(1.) The "Association" means "THE BRITISH MARINE MUTUAL INSURANCE ASSOCIATION, LIMITED."

(2.) "Member." A member means a member of such Association.

(3.) "These presents" means and includes these Articles of Association; and the Articles, Rules, and Regulations of the Association from time to time in force.

(4.) "Committee" means the Committee from time to time of the Association, or as the context may require the Committee assembled at a meeting.

(5.) "Managers" means the Managers from time to time of the Association, and includes each individual member of the co-partnership firm for the time being of the Manager or Managers of the Association.

The front page of the Memorandum and Articles of Association of 1876. They were signed by seven subscribers, one of whom was Joseph Benbrick Foley whose ship, the DUKE OF EDINBURGH, was the first to be entered in the Association for Hull and Materials Insurance.

However, frequent and heavy losses during the War of American Independence bankrupted many and left the shipowner unpaid.

The provincial owner felt particularly vulnerable during this period. His distance from London and the difficulties in communications at that time undermined his confidence in a system that relied so heavily on that city. It was difficult in Newcastle or Liverpool to form an opinion of the solvency and trustworthiness of the metropolitan underwriters who had had among their number from time to time their share of gamblers and incompetents. Further he had to rely on brokers for his dealings with the city men and some of them were famed more for the high level of their commissions than for the excellence of their services.

All of this gave impetus to the movement in the provinces towards self-help. It is perhaps to the owners of the colliers of Newcastle, the Shields and Whitby that the prize goes for fully developing and applying the mutual principle to their operations, although this would risk giving offence to the fishermen of Devon and Cornwall. The mood for change was not confined to these areas alone and associations were also formed in London, despite their proximity to the market offered by Lloyd's and the chartered companies, and elsewhere. By the end of the 18th century around twenty clubs were offering mutual insurance for hulls.

"A calm sea and a prosperous voyage" was always the wish of shipowner and seaman alike. This view, taken aloft on the GARTHSNAID (built as the "Inversnaid" in 1892), conveys the sentiment exactly. The "Garth" fleet, which was owned by Sir William Garthwaite, who purchased most of his fleet secondhand during the First World War, were all entered in British Marine. (National Maritime Museum, Greenwich)

This was underwriting at its most basic. The associations seldom had any working capital. The entry call, which was the same for all, may be likened to a deposit and provided what little cash there was to operate the business. Running costs were kept to a minimum and the claims were paid for by the members directly and usually retrospectively. And a characteristic, still seen today in the organisation of mutual clubs, that of management by a small committee of members, developed. Above all there was no profit margin built into the premium so that the cost of insurance was in theory kept to a minimum. The inevitable outcome, since the 'entry' premium was the same for all, was that unless membership was carefully controlled, the good owner subsidised the inefficiency of the bad. Local knowledge of the owner, his ships and the trades that he was embarked upon were a subjective but necessary qualification of entry to a club. This was a reason why the clubs proliferated on regional, trade or class of ship basis. They must have offered more immediate and/or cheaper insurance than Lloyd's or the two incorporated companies or they would not have grown and prospered.

However there was some doubt about the legitimacy of these early clubs as to whether their establishment was in contravention of the Charters of 1720 which had in effect given legal status only to Lloyd's and the Royal Exchange and the London Assurance. This question, amongst other insurance matters, was considered by a Parliamentary Select Committee set up in 1810. It was felt that if the shipowner had been driven to a course of action for his own protection by the restrictions of the law then the law should be changed. Much criticism was levelled at Lloyd's (accusations of inefficiency and insolvency) and the monopoly of the two charter companies. However attempts to repeal the law of marine insurance failed to get sufficient parliamentary support. The monopoly protection was eventually withdrawn in 1824, after which a number of new proprietary companies entered the insurance market although it was not until the middle of the century that the number of specialist marine companies really expanded, in part due to problems being encountered by the early mutual clubs with their mixture of 'good' and 'bad' members. Six companies were launched in 1859 alone and a further six, which survive in some form today were founded between 1860 and 1864, a survival rate of 50%. Soon after this time Edward Evans was to go into the business of managing mutual marine clubs, among which was one of the name of British Marine Mutual Insurance Association.

ARCTIC STREAM, built at Port Glasgow in 1885, eventually became a total loss after breaking away from her tow near Tynemouth (England) in 1914. (National Maritime Museum, Greenwich)

The abolition of the monopoly held by Lloyd's and the two charter companies meant increased competition for the mutuals from the new companies. They began to offer lower rates through improvements in their operations and by more sophisticated underwriting. The better owners started to find that they could obtain cheaper insurance and better service from the new market and they left the old mutuals which began to go into a downward spiral. They were left with the older less well maintained ships that could get no insurance elsewhere. As a result more and more claims fell on ever decreasing funds and some associations became infamous as the 'rust-bucket clubs'. They had hastened their own

---

Claim: "A Fulsome Report"
Below is an example of the terse reporting that can make a study of the records a frustrating experience. The account hardly does justice to what must have been a voyage of epic proportions.

"ARCTIC STREAM, (Iron sailing ship, built 1885, 1584 g.r.t.), East London (South Africa) to Port Pirie (Australia) in ballast, thence to Silloth (England) with wheat. Heavy weather, yards sprung, decks strained, struck submerged wreckage and galley caught fire and damaged the deck and gear. Paid out £185."

decline, in some instances by departing from the principle of insuring on the basis of local knowledge. In attempting to grow, either for the perceived advantages of size itself or so that the managers could increase their commissions paid on premiums gathered, the clubs began to insure ships from other ports and trades with a consequent loss of control over the quality of the new entrants. Rating ships equally with low advance premiums was at best speculative and frequently difficulties were experienced in collecting the necessary supplementary payments, particularly from owners far afield. As a result of these factors many mutual hull clubs closed in the mid-19th century.

BRITMEX 4 at Southampton, was one of a series of early oil tankers which were entered in British Marine, unlike OLYMPIC, seen in the background. BRITMEX 4 was built at Harland and Wolff, Belfast in 1920 for the British Mexican Petroleum Co. Ltd. (Laurence Dunn Collection)

But shipowners' desire to seek mutual protection for their ships was to be given a new impetus by the growing burden of legislation that was to be enacted in the United Kingdom in the second half of the 19th century. The early mutual clubs were for the insurance of hulls and equipment only but the new laws left the shipowner open to risks other than the physical damage to his property. The need to buy protection from these provided the mutuals with the opportunity to widen the scope of their activities. Another factor was that the testing of the quality of marine insurance policies in the courts sometimes found them wanting and new types of policies were tailored to meet the changing circumstances.

In 1836 it was held in the dispute between De Vaux and Salvador that the standard marine policy of the day did not cover all the liabilities of an owner arising out of a collision. LA VALEUR had collided with FORBES in the Hooghly River (India) with considerable damage to both vessels. After arbitration in Calcutta, both ships were required to bear half of the combined repair costs. LA VALEUR, whose repair costs were the lesser of the two, had to pay a balance to the other and incur the expense of her own crew while under repair. Underwriters refused to reimburse either of these last two items and their stance was upheld by the courts. The fact that LA VALEUR caused more damage than she suffered and paid out accordingly was not held to be a peril of the sea for which she was insured but to be a payment that grew out of "an arbitrary provision in the law of nations from views of general expediency, not as dictated by natural justice, - and can be no more charged on underwriters than a penalty incurred by

Kelly of Belfast's MAY of 1927. John Kelly and Co. were one of British Marine's oldest members, their entries dating from the 1920's until they withdrew from shipowning in the 1980's.

contravention of the revenue laws - ."

This arbitrary provision had been around for a long time. The ancient Sea Laws of Oleron, which dated from the 12th century, had set the precedent out quite clearly and logically. What should happen in the case of a collision so that malpractices would be discouraged, was as follows:

> "In this case the whole damage is to be in common, and to be equally divided and appraised half by half; And the Master and the Mariners of the vessel that struck or grappled with the other, are bound to swear on the holy Evangelist, that they did it not wittingly or wilfully. And the reason why this judgement was first given, was, That an old decayed Vessel might not purposely be put in the way of a better, which will the rather be prevented when they know the damage must be divided"

As a result of this there evolved in 1854 the 'three-fourths running down clause' which limited underwriters' liability to 75% of the cost of any claim arising from a collision. Since 1745 no owner had been allowed to insure for more than his hull value. This meant that potentially a large exposure, like that of LA VALEUR, existed and they formed mutual clubs to protect themselves for these residual liabilities. What was involved was more than just the straightforward physical damage of a collision and Collision Clubs were formed to take account of these new potential liabilities. Around this nucleus they started to insure against such additional risks as wreck removal, quarantine and cargo damage expenses. The mutuals were back in business again and many of the old hull mutuals were revived for what was soon being called 'Protection' insurance.

In the period 1846-56 three pieces of legislation exposed the British shipowner to newly defined responsibilities and he went to his Protection Club looking for new and improved cover. A Limitation of Liability Act fixed the liability of all ships at a maximum of £15 per ton, but without regard to the actual value of the vessel so that expenses above this figure caused heartache for the isolated shipowner and he looked to mutuality for comfort. The Fatal Accidents Act made employers responsible for acts of negligence that caused death in their workforce, and that included seamen. This additional risk had to be insured and where better than in the clubs? New powers were given to Harbour Authorities to sue for damage even if there was no fault on the part of the shipowner. In 1870 in two cases, those of the WESTHOPE and the EMILY, owners lost claims by cargo owners for deviation from contracted destination and for faulty navigation that made them seek insurance cover to indemnify them against such claims in the future. And so the word Indemnity came to added to the word Protection in the names of the mutuals offering these services.

British Marine insured the world's first all welded ship, Anchor-Brocklebank Line's FULLAGAR. Electric welding was by the Quasi-Arc process and the saving of metal in the joints was claimed as an advantage. Her construction received the approval of Lloyd's Register of Shipping and it was noted that "the vessel floated perfectly dry on the occasion of her launch --- and during subsequent operations and machinery trials has given no cause for anxiety." She was also novel for a British ship in her machinery arrangement, having an opposed-piston engine. The type became known as the Cammellaird-Fullagar after Cammell, Laird and Co., the engine builder. (Merseyside Maritime Museum)

But as a result of a dispute that had arisen three years earlier the clubs had faced a bigger challenge when a court ruling eventually invalidated all their mutual policies.

The liquidator of the Arthur Average Association for British Foreign and Colonial Ships had a case against a member who refused to pay up on the winding up of the Association disallowed by the courts. As if this was not bad enough the Master of the Rolls decided that the association had no legal standing because it was not registered under the Companies Act of 1862. (As it had to be, being an association of more than twenty persons.) He said:

> "No contract for sea insurance shall be valid unless the same is expressed in a policy - and every policy shall specify the names of the subscribers or underwriters - and in the case of any of the above mentioned particulars shall be omitted in any policy, such policy shall be null and void to all intents and purposes."

In other words the Arthur Average, or any other mutual not registered under the Companies Act, could not issue policies on behalf of the mutual members unless all of those members signed every policy document. This was a completely impractical proposition.

This judgement was handed down in late June 1875. The mutuals quickly took stock of their situation and they rushed to incorporate themselves. The 'Post Magazine and Insurance Monitor' of 11th March 1876 recorded the incorporation of twenty-nine mutual clubs and among the number was the British Marine Mutual Insurance Association Ltd. It was limited by guarantee to £5 and there were seven subscribers who formed the first committee of the Association. The sole managers, resident at 5 New London Street, were E.R. Evans and Company.

The KIRKELLA (1952) belonged to J. Marr and Son of Hull who were long-time members of the United Kingdom Trawlers Mutual. G.A. Marr was chairman of the U.K.T.M. at the time of the amalgamation with British Marine.

A view of the fish market at Hull, the famous fishing port on England's East Coast, which was the home of the United Kingdom Trawlers Mutual club.

The Medway sailing barge CABBY was not insured by British Marine but has the distinction of being the venue of a Board Meeting while cruising in the Solent in July 1991. She is owned, and beautifully maintained, by Crescent Shipping Ltd., which company, in the days when it was known as London and Rochester Trading Co. Ltd., operated many such fine craft. British Marine had a long connection with the Medway barge trade and put up a cup in 1958 for their annual series of match races.

London and Rochester under its original name and those of Crescent Shipping Ltd. and Hays Marine Services Ltd. has provided the Association with a remarkable continuity of service on its Committees and Board. Beginning with E.A. Gill (1909-53) and following on with M.O. Gill (1953-74), G.S.C. Clarabut (1974-82), P.D.T. Roberts (1982-85) and A.R. Winter (1985-93) we have a continuous period of eighty-four years. In the absence of any other information to the contrary it is likely that the company is the oldest and longest entered member of the British Marine.

The Early Days

At the time of the incorporation Edward Reid Evans was managing seven mutual clubs and they all came under the umbrella of the name of the British Marine Mutual Insurance Association Ltd. He had started in the mutual insurance business with a club for sailing ships and there is in the records a letter on the headed notepaper of the British Marine of 1888, which carries the legend 'For Sailing Ships'. This was certainly the earliest of his clubs going back to 'at least 1869' to quote the Board minutes of nearly a century later when an attempt was made to establish the age of the Association.

Evans was from Northern stock, the Reids, his mother's family, had for centuries been farmers from the Haddington area, near Edinburgh in Scotland. The Evans family hailed from Berwick, in the North-East corner of England and were on the Roll of Burgesses of that town in 1603. However it was in London, where his mother was born, that Edward Reid Evans' parents met and married. His father had been born in Berwick and it is not certain why they had migrated South. Not much is known either of Evans early career in business but we know that he was made a Freeman of the City of London in 1875. This honour was not bestowed on those who were not men of substance nor well established and respected in the commercial community. We may take it then that his probity and expertise in the field of marine underwriting and brokerage, for there was little distinction made between the two activities at that time, went back some way.

Edward Reid Evans, who set up British Marine in the 1860's and managed it from its incorporation in 1876 until his death in 1901.

Another clue to the date of 'birth' of the business is in the name of one of the seven, the hull club known as the British Iron Club. Iron as a material of hull construction had been used experimentally around 1814. Tod and McGregor had started building in iron on the Clyde commercially in 1834 and by 1853 they had stopped wooden construction altogether. Steel replaced iron totally within 30 years but the 1850/60's was the period in Britain when the demand for a club specialising in the insurance of ships built in this new fangled material would have grown. To move with the times Evans would have to have recognised this trend. He would also have been aware that 1873 was the year in which British yards built as many steamers as they did sailing ships for British owners. (The tonnage of the steamers was 234,000 while that of the sailing ships was only 187,000.)

Iron hulls were the link for three of the main hull classes. The British Iron, known as Class 1, was distinguished from the Iron General (Class 2) by different financial limits and allowable geographical trading areas. Class 3, the Iron Freights Club, was for "all averages and loss of freights" for the previous two classes.

Class 4, the British A1, was as chauvinistic in its entry conditions as its name suggests and the British Marine Mutual or Class 5, which was subdivided into four separately rated groups, was for British ships (including coasters) of different ages and non-British classifications. The British General was a catch-all club (Class 6), whose ratings were fixed by the decisions of the Committee and was generally for hulls that did not qualify for any of the other classes. Finally, Class 7, the British Freight, serviced these non-iron clubs much as Class 3 did for Classes 1 and 2. These were the classes into which the British coasting trade and the wooden hulled sailing ships entered.

In effect, all seven classes, whatever their individual characteristics, allowed the shipowner to choose to trade where he wished, even on a world-wide basis. Their class rules were fully specified and linked to the Articles of the British Marine Mutual Association Ltd. All classes were supervised by a committee of members.

There was also a separate agreement with E.R. Evans and Company for the

The Class 2 Accounts for the 1907/08 year. These demonstrate the method of calculation of the call for this class. The total of £1090 would be paid by each owner in proportion to that part of the contributing capital he had entered. Note the large number of settlements for Workmen's Compensation.

management of the Association. The preamble tells us that Evans had "for some years past established certain mutual insurance associations" but sadly is not specific as to how many years. His company was allowed commissions of 0.25% on the premiums of Classes 1 to 4 and 0.375% on Classes 5 to 7 subject to a minimum of one guinea or £1.05 in today's terms.

A rather different view of the GARTHSNAID from that on page 13 and one which illustrates dramatically the hardships and dangers being afloat in a sailing ship in a gale in the Southern Ocean. (National Maritime Museum, Greenwich)

Essentially these seven classes provided two services, hull and freight insurance for four main types of ship: iron hulled steamers and wooden, composite and iron built sailing ships. When the hull class of 1996, accommodating nearly 3000 ships of considerable variety, is contemplated today there is a sense of amazement that five classes were considered necessary to distinguish between the various forms of hull insurance in the 1870's and that they required two freight classes to service them.

There were two main reasons for this diversity. The first was the mutual principle of like co-habiting with like. Sailing owners no doubt preferred to share the risks of others who favoured canvas rather than steam. The methods and the technology were well understood and had been tested over centuries whereas iron and steam were only just beginning to prove themselves. The second was that the 'Art' of underwriting had not then evolved to the sophisticated 'Science' of today. The columns of the various Insurance periodicals frequently carried pleas for the pooling of underwriting results and there were many criticisms of the performance and methods of reporting profit and loss in the proprietary marine insurance companies in the 1860's. In the years 1860-64 twelve proprietary companies contrived to make an aggregate profit (seven of them reported a loss) of £104,000 on premium income of £6,933,000. Eleven of these, for one had gone into liquidation, lost an aggregate sum of £29,700 in 1868 and none of the new proprietary companies which came to the market between 1865 and 1869 survived 1871. Clearly the mutuals, who charged the 'right' premium, i.e. that based on actual claim costs, offered the greater security at that time.

AMIRAL CECILLE, a three-masted steel sailing ship, built 1902 for the Compagnie de Navigation Francaise, was one of the French entrants that were the mainstay (pun intended) of the membership of Class 1 in the early 20th century. (San Francisco Maritime National Historical Park)

British Marine's freight clubs had the same rules, albeit applied to different hull classes but the variety in regulation built into the hull clubs was considerable. Today's Hull and Machinery class has one set of rules to which the underwriter applies his rate depending on a range of circumstances and claims experience, but in 1876 there was a clear intention to build the rating into the rules of the individual classes. In Class 5 rates varying between 6% and 12% were charged depending on classification at Lloyd's Register of Shipping and the 12% rate applied to all Class 6 ships. Entry to the British A1 Club depended on having at least a nine year classification (the standard was lower for Class 6) but there was a 50% deductible for trading in timber in the Baltic between September and April. This was only 10% if you were a member of Class 2 where the classification requirements were either 100A1 or 90A1, but then you could not trade to Hudson Bay or Greenland.

The premier Club was the British Iron which demanded the highest standards but gave world-wide trading freedom specifically for the Southern Trades and the crossing of the Equator. However even in this select group the underwriter asked for a deductible of £20% on claims while trading to East London (South Africa), the West Indies and the Spanish Main (sic) in the months from August to March.

Inevitably this led to a plethora of rule alterations as circumstances changed, and there was scarcely an Annual General Meeting for the next thirty years that did not have resolutions for rule alterations, some of them quite inconsequential, put to the members for consideration. Not so inconsequential was the decision, hotly debated at the time in 1887, to allow brokers to be paid 5% commission on estimated premiums for introductions.

In 1878 Class 4 entry was restricted to British ships and a new Class 5 for British and Colonial vessels was introduced. It only lasted four years. More significantly, a Protection Club, Class 8, was constituted for loss of life, improper navigation, one fourth collision costs and damage to docks and piers. The move towards providing full P.&.I. as we know it today had begun. The process was completed in 1886 when the scope of Class 8 was increased "to cover what is usually called Indemnity". And so it went on through the remainder of the 19th century with the changes reflecting the developing technology of the shipping industry. Classes came and went with frequent re-numberings. Steel hulls were recognised in 1887 and composites were then excluded. In 1894 the class for wooden hulled sailing ships was closed and the whole Association rationalised into four main classes, Hulls (the British Iron for which a separate committee was set up), P.&.I., Defence and Collision. This broadly is the form that the

Association has today. However Evans set up two new clubs under his management control in 1907, the Metropolitan Marine Mutual and the Central Marine Mutual, both associations for coasting sailing vessels. They were not part of British Marine.

Sailing ships continued to be of prime interest for many years and there were still entries of this type of vessel until at least 1935 and probably up to the start of the Second World War. British Marine managers took part with those of other clubs in annual conferences on underwriting matters affecting this type of vessel until at least the First World War. At this distance their discussions on ratings seem to come to intriguing conclusions which there is not time or space to research fully here. Why was only guano from Chile or Peru acceptable as a cargo? Why were the West Coast South American ports known as "the seven bad ports" and considered unsafe? At least the decision to insist on top masts, top-gallants and all back-stays being renewed on twelve year old ships is understandable and sensible.

Minutes

RELATING TO

THE FIFTH CONFERENCE OF DIRECTORS & MANAGERS

OF

Mutual Associations for the Insurance of Hulls, &c. of Sailing Vessels.

HELD IN THE

LIVERPOOL STREET HOTEL, LONDON,

On Tuesday, the 8th day of November, 1910, at 2.30 o'clock p.m.

OBJECT OF MEETING.—To confer together with a view of arranging for adoption by the Mutual Clubs represented at the Conference an uniform Policy as regards Clauses, Warranties and Conditions.

Present.—Messrs. A. Bilbrough ; Harry J. Boxsius ; John R. Campbell ; John S. De Wolf ; Robt. R. Douglas ; Jno. Edgar ; V. W. Evans ; F. Y. Finch ; Geo. Grant ; T. G. Hardie ; D. J. Hughes ; John Joyce ; William Lewis ; Fred J. Miners ; Walter Patterson ; A. Pears ; Arthur J. Preston ; Wm. Price ; John Rae ; A. F. Rolph ; Samuel Roberts ; R. J. Rowat ; Robt. J. Thomas ; R. R. Thomas ; Wm. Thomas ; James A. Young. Also, for purpose of consultation if required, Wm. Clifton (William A. Crump & Son), and Arthur Lindley (Robert Lindley, Sons & Davison).

Chairman.—It was proposed by Mr. William Lewis, seconded by Mr. John R. Campbell, and carried, that Mr. A. Bilbrough be appointed Chairman of this Conference.

Minutes.—The Minutes of the last Conference, held in Liverpool, on 5th November, 1909, having been duly printed and circulated, were taken as read and confirmed.

Voting.—It was decided that the Voting be confined to the Directors, and that the Managers do not, therefore, vote.

The minutes of the Fifth Conference on Sailing Ships of 1910. Victor Evans and Harry Boxsius represented British Marine and another well-known name in mutual management, Arthur Bilbrough, chaired the proceedings. This Conference decided that no payment would be made for the loss of sails or running gear unless "--- they be so damaged or lost by the loss or giving way of spars or standing rigging, or by stranding, sinking, collision or fire."

In response to the passing of the Workmen's Compensation Act (W.C.A.), the P.&.I. Club included cover for injuries to crew in 1907. This practically became a class within a class as members could buy P.&.I. without W.C.A. cover and did not have to contribute to calls arising out of such claims. Just how much this protection was needed is evidenced by the example that in one period in 1908/09 W.C.A. claims accounted for 50% of the value and 70% of the number of the claims paid in the whole P.&.I. class. Social attitudes had clearly changed as twenty years earlier British Marine had joined with others "to protect the members against unreasonable demands or actions of labour combinations affecting the shipping trade." But then that was what the Association was all about, reflecting the changing technological and social needs of it's membership.

The Association had by that time developed a shape that is recognisable today. There were four distinct classes providing a specific risk insurance service for unspecified types of ship. The rules were becoming general and the rating of the individual entries was becoming more detailed and sophisticated. This was the situation that pertained up to the start of the 1914-18 War when the opening of hostilities created the necessity for a fifth class, War Risks.

An early 20th century scene of the steel barque GENERAL DE NEGRIER, entered in 1902 by N. and C. Guillion, loading grain at Oakland (U.S.A.). Such bulky, relatively low value, cargoes were the staple diet of the sailing ships at this time and sustained their commercial viability until the 1930's. Many such vessels were entered in British Marine. (San Francisco Maritime National Historical Park)

*An early oil tanker,
PASS OF LENY
(built 1922), of the
fleet of the Bulk Oil
Shipping Co. Ltd.,
which were entered
in British Marine
from 1922 to 1946.*

HOOTACT (R.
Lapthorn and Co.
Ltd.) typifies the
1950's coasters that
were members of
the Association.

A launch from the Furness Shipyard on the Tees in 1951 shows three forms of propulsion, screw, paddle and oar. (Today the men in the wherry would not be allowed to go afloat without life jackets !) LINGDALE, a fine example of a twin-stack paddle tug, was built in 1882 and purchased by Tees Towing Co. Ltd. in 1914. She went for breaking up three years after this photograph was taken. She was considered valuable enough to be entered for Class V, War Risks, in 1939 at the age of 57 and after 25 years in the ownership of Tees. (J.H. Proud)

The steam tug BANBURY CROSS (built on the Clyde in 1945 as a wartime fleet auxiliary and purchased by Tees Towing Co. Ltd. in 1950) is pictured going to the aid of the aptly named GRIPFAST off the north-east coast of England. Tugs are one type of Class 1 entry that cannot be discouraged from putting themselves in hazardous situations. (J.H. Proud)

"Free of Capture and Seizure"

War posed special problems for ship insurance in the 20th century when the essentially non-combatant merchant marine was thrust into the frontline of hostilities in an entirely unique manner.

Merchantmen had always been fair game for the warships and privateers of warring nations and underwriters had historical experience to fall back on in the event of an outbreak of hostilities. The standard Lloyd's policy, which all of the mutuals followed to a greater or lesser extent, was quite specific that cover was offered for times of peace and that separate considerations applied in time of war. As the wording put it a vessel's insurance was warranted " - free from capture, seizure and detention - and also from all consequences of hostilities or warlike operations - ". This was popularly known as the F.C.&.S. Clause. It would appear to have been used in the times of Britain's conflicts with Napoleonic France and was intended to avoid paying out on claims that resulted from the increased hazards of wartime as well as direct attack by an enemy.

The clause was famously tested by the Hatteras Light case in 1863 during the American Civil War. The IONIDES stranded, it was claimed, as the direct result of the light on Cape Hatteras being extinguished by the troops of the Confederacy, and that a claim under war insurances should be allowed. This was resisted by the insurance company in question, not a mutual, and the case went to court. There the view was taken that normal marine risks were not converted into war risks because of the absence of lighthouses or, to extend the principle of the duty of care placed on the ship's master, because vessels sailed without lights, adopted zig-zag courses or sailed close to other vessels (in convoy, for example) to avoid the possibility of attack. This grey area was to persist until the 1939-1945 war and clouded the interpretation of which insurance covered many war-time incidents. The British Government acted to provide cover in the 1914-18 conflict and did so in a variety of forms, one of which came to involve British Marine in 1917.

Both the Crimean War (1854-56) and the Franco-Prussian War (1871) had increased the shipowner's awareness of his lack of cover and from time to time some of the P.&.I. clubs, but not British Marine, which did not get into the business of owners' risks until 1878, had offered cover not available because of the F.C.&.S. clause. The cover was often on a pooled basis as the individual clubs felt too exposed when standing alone. Fiscal changes in the United Kingdom, and perhaps some anticipation of troubled times ahead, encouraged the formation of War Risk Clubs in 1912. Consequently when a British Government committee, which convened in April 1914, considered the problems of marine insurance in time of war, it looked to the War Risk Clubs for co-operation in the provision of cover.

The agreement, drawn up in July 1914, this time definitely in anticipation of the outbreak of hostilities, was based on the Government re-insuring 80% of the hull values of all vessels entered in the War Risk Clubs on premiums fixed between the Clubs and the Government. The rates were fixed for single or round-trip voyages or for a maximum period of ninety-one days so that changing underwriting experience on claims could be rapidly reflected in changes in premiums. Indeed at one stage in 1917, when shipping losses reached a peak of 545,000 tons in one month, the premiums of £6% were quadruple those of 1914. A War Risks Mutual had been set up at the beginning of the War for British fishing vessels with the Government taking 80% re-insurance. In principle the concern was that supplies of raw materials and foods should be protected in the national interest by ensuring that all ships engaged in these vital trades should not be prevented from sailing due the absence of adequate insurance cover for the undoubted risks involved. The principle was extended to the ships of allied and neutral nations, including sailing ships, which brought cargoes to Britain. Cargo insurance was also available through the State Insurance Office which was opened in London for this purpose.

In practice there were difficulties in the operation of the scheme and there were anomalies in the different treatments of ships which were requisitioned by the

The British Iron Club policy document of 1907. Note the restrictions placed on, for example, operating in the Baltic between October and March. Highlighted is the famous war risks exception clause "Warranted nevertheless free of capture, seizure and detention."

Government and those which were trading in the 'normal' way. The War Risk Clubs had to make supplementary calls on their 20% lines for the three years 1915-1917 as the premiums were inadequate to cover expenses for administration, which were carried by the Clubs, and the losses incurred. Eventually the Government decided to take 100% of the risk when it introduced

Built in 1883, the iron hulled J.T.NORTH, was named after the 'Nitrate King', so called for his entrepreneurial activities in the nitrate trade in Chile. Entered in British Marine for Hull and Materials cover. Under Danish ownership she became a war casualty in December 1916. (National Maritime Museum Greenwich)

the convoy system in 1917. At the same time it extended its involvement to the re-insurance of coasters and this brought British Marine directly into the system for the first time.

The arrangement with British Marine, which came into effect on the half year at 20th August 1917, was a 70% re-insurance with the Club taking the balance of the risk. The Association also took 100% of some hulls resulting in approximately 40% of the total risk in the book, in what became Class 5, falling on British Marine. The rate was fixed at £6% because of the huge losses being experienced at that time but it had fallen to £0.5% after the Armistice in 1918. In the period to the end of the War the Association recorded thirteen losses and three damages of entered ships. The result was that a surplus was created. All the records show that the First World War was a profitable period for insurance with Lloyd's, where an open market continued throughout, and the proprietary companies making profits.

The statement of account for Class 5 for the half year to 20th February 1918, showed a positive balance of £3759 on a net income (after paying 70% of the premium to the Government) of £11,357. This figure included interest on money from premiums placed on deposit or invested in War Bonds. The committee was deeply concerned about the proper way to proceed after this unexpected state of affairs. As mutualists they knew that profit making was not the purpose of the Association and they instinctively felt that the surplus should be returned to the members. The wording of the class rules made it quite clear that additional calls could be made to meet the costs of claims if these exceeded the original calls but the disposal of surpluses was not specifically contemplated in the text. Counsel's opinion was sought. The terms in which he couched his advice and the principles of mutuality which he set out are worth recording in full. After considering the Class rules he was unequivocal in his view that:

> "It follows in my opinion that the surplus falls to be divided among the members of the class in their capacity as underwriters. The division should be on equitable principles, the guiding principle being that the members should be on an equal basis and the division an equal one in exact proportion to their liabilities as underwriters. This means in my opinion that the division must take into account the total amount entered in the class, the amount entered by each member and the time during which he was liable to contribute."

It followed that a member liable at any time during a year, and not just for a full year, would be entitled to a share in the surplus. Consequently the Association paid back to the membership on the basis of £2.0% for 1918 and £5.5% for 1919. Prudently it was decided to buy re-insurance for the run-off for the larger values in the class.

Claim: "The Royal Navy to the Rescue"
The motor schooner STASIA (built 1917, 1564 g.r.t.) was lying at the International Dock, Shanghai, completing repairs and making ready for sea, when at 07.00hrs a fire broke out in the engine room. Thereupon to prevent oil in the tanks from taking fire the vessel was scuttled by gunfire by a British Gunboat for the safety of the port.
  The ship was subsequently raised and repaired. The owners unsuccessfully sued the Shanghai Dock and Engineering Company, who had been working on the vessel, claiming that their negligence caused the fire.The case was appealed to the Privy Council who upheld the judgement of the Supreme Court of Shanghai. British Marine paid all the repair and legal costs having approved of the member's decision to take the Dockyard to law.

Not the STASIA but a reproduction made from the General Arrangement drawing of her sister ship COMMANDENT DE ROCI (Laurence Dunn)

As suggested above British Marine was not the only underwriter to make a surplus in those last fifteen months of the War when losses fell dramatically. With Government taking 70% of British Marine's premium and 100% elsewhere it was bound to have paid out less on claims than it collected if its experience was remotely similar to that of the Association. In fact the British Government made a massive £26,000,000 profit on a fixed premium income of £197,800,000. Money was lost on British sailing ships and fishing vessels and on cargo in British bottoms but the insurance of the hulls of British steamers produced a profit of £11,000,000. The whole of the credit balance did not belong to the British and substantial sums were returned to the Belgian, French and Italian authorities. Nonetheless some £17,000,000 was kept. No attempt was made to repay this sum to the owners of the vessels. The Government had agreed to ships being insured at increased values in recognition of the rate at which replacement building costs had risen during the war but even then this significant surplus was still made.

While no calls were made in Class 5 after 1921, because there were no claims, entry fees were charged and there were still 183 vessels entered in 1923. In fact, despite the cessation of European hostilities, the class did not close although it only had 83 ships entered in 1935. This trebled in 1936 with the commencement of the Spanish Civil War when the class became active again and charged premiums.

GOVERNMENT WAR INSURANCE SCHEME.

Preliminary Statement of Results.

These figures are provisional and subject to correction as and when the claims for outstanding losses have been presented.

Scheme.	Premium. £	Losses. £	Balance. £
1. Hulls of British steamers ...	78,930,000	62,800,000	+ 16,130,000
2. Hulls of British steamers trading to Holland ...	403,000	620,000	— 217,000
3. Hulls of British sailing ships ...	42,000	133,000	— 91,000
4. Hulls and gear of British fishing vessels..	428,000	1,424,000	— 996,000
5. Hulls of British coasting vessels ...	133,000	72,000	+ 61,000
6. Hulls of Norwegian steamers (old scheme) ...	25,000,000	23,000,000	+ 2,000,000
7. Hulls of Norwegian steamers (new scheme) ...	4,800,000	1,300,000	+ 3,500,000
8. Hulls of Norwegian steamers (excess values) ...	2,000,000	750,000	+ 1,250,000
9. Hulls and cargo of other neutral steamers ...	8,500,000	7,200,000	+ 1,300,000
10. Hulls of British steamers in French coal trade ...	735,000	581,000	+ 154,000
11. Hulls of Belgian steamers ...	1,406,000	1,196,000	+ 210,000
12. Hulls of Belgian fishing vessels ...	17,100	1,600	+ 15,500
13. Hulls of Roumanian steamers ...	33,000	100,000	— 67,000
14. Cargo in British steamers (old scheme) ...	48,500,000	59,500,000	—11,000,000
15. Cargo in British sailing ships (old scheme) ...	140,000	688,000	— 548,000
16. Cargo in British and neutral steamers and British sailing ships (new scheme).	11,500,000	8,000,000	+ 3,500,000
17. Cargo in British coasting vessels ...	25,700	92,700	— 67,000
18. Cargo in Belgian steamers ...	1,070,000	170,000	+ 900,000
19. Cargo in Roumanian steamers ...	61,000	425,000	— 364,000
20. Cargo in British steamers—Marine Insurance ...	141,000	19,500	+ 121,500
21. Seamen's effects ...	89,000	384,000	— 295,000
22. Canteen and officers' mess stock in H.M. Ships..	55,800	36,000	+ 19,800
23. Aircraft and bombardment...	13,610,000	2,970,000	+10,640,000
24. Aircraft and bombardment (Egyptian cotton) ...	7,200	—	+ 7,200
25. Miscellaneous...	171,000	—	+ 171,000
Totals ...	197,797,800	171,462,800	+26,335,000

The whole of this credit balance of over 26 millions does not belong to the British Government. The profits made on the Belgian schemes (Nos. 11 and 18) are for the account of the Belgian Government, and a considerable portion of the profits made on the various neutral schemes are for the account of the French and Italian Governments. The profit on Scheme 10 is for the account of the French Government. This will reduce the total credit balance by about one-third, leaving something like 17 millions to the credit of the British Government.

Short explanatory notes on the various schemes are appended.

Scheme 1.

This is an extract from the preliminary statement of results, published in 1919, of the Government War Risks Insurance Schemes. A substantial underwriting profit of £26 million was made which was reduced to £17 million when monies had been returned to Belgian, French and Italian governments. The only really substantial loss was made on insuring cargoes in British steamers.

The unchanging face of the British coaster. Kelly's BALMARINO (above) of 1889 and KERRYMORE (below) of 1921 look remarkably similar despite the thirty year gap in their ages. The older ship was not scrapped until 1957, only a year before her much younger sister.

In November 1938 British Marine approached the Board of Trade to discuss what proportion of risk it might be asked to assume in the event of hostilities breaking out. The answer was to be 20%. Unlike the 1914-18 conflict British Marine was to be involved from the very beginning as the Government decided to cover the whole range of shipping activity in its wartime insurance planning. An agreement between the Association and the Government came into force on the outbreak of war in September 1939 and the Government assumed responsibility for 80% of the risk and took 80% of the premium for all entered tonnage. There were two main types of cover, hull and machinery and freight and disbursements. At no time in this war did the British Marine carry a 100% risk on any vessel and indeed as Government policy developed during the conflict it became merely an administrator in some instances as all of the risk and all of the premiums were taken by the Ministry of War Transport. The number of ships covered in the Club quickly rose to three hundred with an insured value of £2,840,000 by December 1939.

It has to be remembered of course that this war risks cover was just that and normal insurance for the usual range of marine risk carried on. This was why the terms of the F.C.&.S. clause continued to be of importance. In many instances disputes arose as to whether or not a casualty had occurred from a marine or war peril, as defined by this clause, and this decided whether the underwriter, like the Association or Lloyd's, paid or the Government. When uncertainties like this occurred British Marine would frequently advance half of the sum in question to its member pending the outcome of the legal wrangle so that to an extent the member was able to get on with his urgent wartime business. The Ministry colluded in this process and quarterly financial adjustments were made between the two bodies throughout the War.

One such dispute affected a British Marine member in 1939. His vessel the mv BRENDONIA (built 1937, 313 g.r.t.) was lying at anchor, showing her anchor light, off Margate (England) when she was run down and sunk by the ss ALDERPOOL, a much larger ship (built 1930, 4313 g.r.t.), which was proceeding without lights. She was on charter to the Government and en route to load supplies for the Army in France. ALDERPOOL was found to be entirely at fault but the claim against her marine underwriter was resisted by him as he maintained that it was a war risk. Notwithstanding the facts of the direction of her employment by the Ministry, the Lord Chief Justice in arbitration decided that it was a marine and not a war risk because the military cargo had not been loaded at the time of the collision.

In all the members of British Marine lost twenty-nine vessels and had one hundred and twenty damaged in the course of the war. In other words around half of the number of ships entered in the Club suffered to a greater or lesser extent. Losses reached a peak in the Association's experience from late 1941 to the Spring of 1943 at a cost of £165,000 or 5.8% of the insured value. At the end of 1942 the Ministry was fixing the premium at £7% for a ninety-one day policy in consequence of the rate of losses. This had fallen to £1% one year later in response to improving circumstances.

The F.C.&.S. clause was redrawn in 1943 after a House of Lords decision on the COXWOLD (built 1938, 1124 g.r.t.) case. This vessel, not a member of British Marine, had been bound from Scotland to Norway in 1940 with military supplies when, in the course of carrying out instructions to manoeuvre by the commodore of the convoy of which she was part, she grounded on rocks off the Scottish

---

Claim: "A Case of Evaporation?"
m.v. CURLER (built 1918, 628 g.r.t.) was bound from Leith (Scotland) to Antwerp (Belgium). The cargo was loaded and the hatches sealed at Leith. The hatches were still fastened when the ship arrived at her destination. After discharge was completed it was found that 195 cases of whisky were missing. The Directors agreed to support the member's action for freight recovery.

island of Skye. It was held that the stranding was not due to negligence of those

COXWOLD
*(World Ship Photo
Library)*

on board the COXWOLD but to the warlike operation in which she was engaged, having regard to where she was bound, what she was carrying and under whose orders she was navigating. There was genuine concern that this ruling would potentially lead to all incidents being redefined as "warlike" and that all marine policies would become redundant. Therefore the clause was redrafted to restrict the meaning of "the consequences of hostilities or warlike operations" and so to clarify the distinction between the two types of cover. That form of wording exists to this day.

The Government's method of paying out on claims is worthy of some comment as it demonstrates that contrary to popular belief the British civil service can learn from experience. During the 1914-18 War concern was expressed that insured values were falling behind replacement costs because of the effects of wartime inflation. This was addressed by increasing war risks insured values but it was felt after the war that too many shipowners had taken the money and quit the business! In 1940 the Government Tonnage Replacement Agreement established a basic or pre-war value for a hull as the sum that would be recovered in the event of a war loss. The difference between that value and its market value or replacement cost was recognised as an "increased value" which was not paid directly to the owner but was put into an interest bearing fund. When, and only when, the owner purchased or built a replacement vessel was the increased value plus any interest earned on it paid to him. There was great debate over many months about the values of ships entered through the British Marine, with Evans and Company valiantly defending the members' interests, and when some of the agreed values exceeded the Association's upper limits on hull values the excess amounts were re-insured with the Britannia Steamship Insurance Association Ltd.

In 1941 the Ministry decided to pay the total premiums for war insurance on all policies in force for requisitioned ships and coasting vessels, thus assuming 100% of the risk, and went further in October that year by paying the premiums directly to the Association. This was to lead to a debate about the "ownership" of credit balances and the costs of administration between the the two parties. This was finally settled in 1949 by the British Marine paying over £160,000. In fact Government created large surpluses in its Marine Insurance Fund as it had done in the 1914-18 period but it could be argued that they found their way into the funding of the post-bellum reconstruction programme and so in that sense the excess premiums were returned to the shipowner.

British Marine had also accumulated some modest surpluses from the days when it had taken 20% of the risk. After the Ministry had terminated the War Risks arrangement in 1947 the Class 5 Committee debated what to do about them and the decision was made to hold them in general reserve for the class.

As it had done after the First World War Class 5 continued in existence and indeed found a renewed purpose in protecting the interest of a member who suffered loss in the troubles of Northern Ireland in 1981. In essence it is still alive today, a favoured protection with many mortgage banks, although its provisions were absorbed into the Class 1, Hull and Machinery, rules in 1990.

EVA WITTE
*(World Ship Photo
Library)*

Claim: "Foam on Troubled Waters"
The mv EVA WITTE (built 1958, 419g.r.t.) was berthed in Swansea when her crews' accommodation was "invaded" by some Indian peddlars intent on selling their wares. They refused to leave when ordered to do so by the ship's master. Not being in the first flush of youth the Captain armed himself with a fire extinguisher to re-inforce his perfectly reasonable request. But as the report of the incident said,

```
"due to the sudden movement of one peddlar the extinguisher went off and a
quantity of foam hit him."
```

The master was charged under the Offences Against the Person Act of 1861 and taken to court. He was acquitted but he incurred legal costs of £32 in defending himself. It was pointed out that no rule of Class 3, Freight, Demurrage and Defense, covered that particular set of circumstances but the Board, when the matter was brought to their notice, had great sympathy for the master and decided to pay the legal costs as long as it was appreciated that the payment was

```
"Not to be taken as establishing any precedent."
```

CASTLETON
*(National Maritime
Museum,
Greenwich)*

Claim: "Typical Voyage"
The barque CASTLETON, (steel sailing ship, built 1891, 2395 g.r.t.) on passage from Port Talbot (Wales) to Antofagasta (Chile) and thence to Hamburg (Germany). These extracts are from the log.

> *2nd June. Left Port Talbot.*
> *24th July. Lost fore top gallant.*
> *28th July. Gale. Lost foresail, main lower topsail and main topmast staysail.*
> *24th August. Gale. Lost upper fore topsail.*
> *31st August. Lost outer jib.*
> *10th September. Discovered forepeak leaking badly. Crew employed pumping.*
> *20th September. Arrived Antofagasta. Discharged. Sailed on 23rd.*
> *15th January. Gale. Lost lower main topgallant sail. Decks straining. Forward house doors burst in, flooding the saloon, destroying fittings and smashing pantry gear. Steering gear damaged.*
> *29th January. Lost two fore topsails.*
> *14th March. Gale. Port lifeboat damaged and starboard one smashed. Sundry damages about decks. Lost upper main topsail.*
> *17th April. Arrived Hamburg.*

The total of the claim was for £772. Claims for sails were not allowed unless the spars and/or rigging and masts were carried away.

Claims

After an experience of dealing with proprietary insurance most people could be forgiven for expecting the attitude of insurers to be "How can I avoid paying this claim?" The philosophy of the committee of directors of a marine mutual, one of whose main tasks in life is to authorise the payment of claims, is rather "How can we deal with this member's problem within the rules of the club?" The current of belief in mutuality, "There but for the grace of God go I!", runs strongly.

It was not always necessarily thus and it would not be accurate to create the impression that the relationship between the member and the Club, or specifically between British Marine and its members, was always free of disagreements. In 1886, for example, a Mr Williams took British Marine to court over a matter of offsetting premiums due against a claim unpaid. He won. Quite rightly, it would seem, to anyone with an instinct for natural justice. He had paid his call for the year in which the claim fell and was owed money for the claim. Since his quarterly instalment for the next year was less than he was due by way of claim settlement it seemed logical to suggest that he did not have to write a cheque in favour of the Club. The managers took a different view but then in those days the income from initial calls was not sufficient to pay claims and indeed was not designed to do so. The judgement went in favour of the member and he bore no grudge and continued to insure his ships with the Club.

The Club's rules for each class of insurance have a catch-all clause, the famous directors' discretion clause. This allows a member to appeal to the Board of the Association in unusual circumstances, and they abound in shipping, when the rules do not quite cover the actual situation found in the incident in question. The directors subscribe to the principle that a member should always act as if he were uninsured but do sympathetically recognise when a member has acted sensibly and prudently to minimise the effects of an incident and yet found himself out of pocket. As practical shipowners they also recognise when another owner may not have been entirely blameless, and act accordingly.

Over zealous interpretation of the rules does not always meet with the approval of the members. As one vocal but well-respected owner, entered in British Marine for many years, put it, "This owner understood that the Association was there to help him and not to shelter behind every rule as theory and practice, particularly at sea in a small ship, can be very different."

The early claims books are endlessly fascinating. The picture that they create of the world of shipping a hundred and more years ago is a revelation and make today's maritime operations seem quite unremarkable and prosaic.

The language of the reports is often laconic. ("Terrific gale. Pigsty broke adrift.") The occasional hyperbole can be forgiven. ("Dinghy broken to atoms.") Written to substantiate the justification of a claim their understatements often have the effect of highlighting the drama of, for example, a South Atlantic gale. Best of all are when the reports include extracts from the master's log.

Not the INVERNESS but the nitrate carrier RELIANCE, on fire at Iquique (Peru). This is very much what the master of the INVERNESS would have seen from his lifeboat when he had to abandon her on fire in mid-Pacific. Another British Marine entrant, MARION FRASER, also burnt out while loading nitrate in October 1910. (National Maritime Museum, Greenwich)

Claim: "The Boy Stood on the Burning Deck"
The following is quoted from the log of the barque INVERNESS (built 1902, 1959 g.r.t.), April, 1918. We know that her cargo was coal (outward bound from Port Natal, South Africa, to Taltal, Chile) and that spontaneous combustion of certain types of coal was not unknown.

"06.00hrs. Strong NW winds and high cross sea. Ship under reefed topsail reefed foresail and lower staysails. Temperature in the main hold 185 degrees Fahrenheit and increasing. (The celsius equivalent is 85 degrees) Got the boats ready for swinging out.
07.00hrs. Steam coming through main ventilator apparently caused by water pipe having melted and water boiling in the tanks.
07.40hrs. Flames coming out through main ventilator. Called all hands and swung the boats out which were fully provisioned. Discovered the main mast settling down and the stays and rigging slackening up. Main mast swaying from side to side. Flames coming out of forward ventilators. deck seams smoking and pitch boiling out. Decided to abandon ship which we did at 08.00hrs.
12.00hrs. Sailed up alongside and remained near the ship until 14.00hrs. Found the main deck smoking fore

INVERNESS in port in happier times and (below) under way. (National Maritime Museum, Greenwich)

and aft and every indication of heavy fire in the mid-ship section. The main mast having settled down considerably and swaying from side to side made it dangerous to approach the ship too close. Then decided it was not safe to board again as by all appearances nothing could be done to save the ship.

Therefore as darkness would soon be coming we shaped course for Rapa Island about 670 miles to the NNE. High sea on but gradually going down and weather moderating.

16.00hrs. Could see the main royal mast and yard falling over and hanging aloft. The lower mast, topmast and gallant mast and yards still standing but swaying heavily. The lower topsails and foresail and lower staysails still being set, the upper topsails having been lowered so as to stop her making way as we lowered the boats, she was heading to the North and East smoking heavily when last seen at 17.30hrs.

19.00hrs. Just before darkness saw the Mate's boat to the Westward one mile. Showed a white light but got no reply. "

 After seven days and nights in open boats the crew arrived at Rapa Island (Pacific Ocean). They remained there for six weeks until a steamer took them to Tahiti. Is it not remarkable that despite the danger of his situation the master continues to log the technical details of his sail plan?

 The claim for the total loss of hull and freight was paid in full.

*GLENESSLIN (built 1882, 1880 g.r.t.), was on passage from Hamburg
(Germany) to Santos (Brazil), with a cargo of cement and her master decided to
take the Eastern route via the Cape of Good Hope because she encountered a
gale Cape Horn. After discharging she was making a ballast passage to
Portland (U.S.A.) when, in poor visibility she struck rocks in Tillamook Bay
and filled with water in September 1913. British Marine paid out on the total
loss value of £6,600 and the expenses of selling the wreck.*

Claims are the very life blood of any marine insurance organisation and no
history would be complete without recognising this. As illustrations of the
business of a mutual Club nothing compares with giving examples of the many
types of claims that have been made over the years. They tell the day-to-day story
of the British Marine as no other facet of the business does. They are better
illustrations than any set of photographs of the ships could ever be. So, dispersed

*MADELEINE
CONSTANCE
(National Maritime
Museum,
Greenwich)*

throughout this book there is a selection, chosen not quite at random, of the ordinary, the dramatic, the amusing and the tragic. In their way they are representative of the most meaningful interface between the member and the Club.

Claim: "A Regular Customer"

Some ships made regular appearances in the claims accounts. They were not badly maintained or managed but they were engaged on hazardous trades and were rated accordingly by British Marine. Such an entry was the barque MADELEINE CONSTANCE (built 1892, 434 g.r.t.). A few of her experiences are described below. They are not the run-of-the-mill bumps and scrapes but they involve some of the principles of marine law beloved to salvors, surveyors, arbitrators and advocates.

In August 1916 she was loading timber at Alligator Pond (Jamaica) when a hurricane hit the area. She was lying to two anchors with additional cables out when she was struck in quick succession by two other ships whose anchors had dragged. Her bowsprit was carried away and the port anchor cable was torn off the windlass, leaving her with only one anchor. The starboard anchor chain eventually snapped and she was driven ashore. On the advice of a salvage surveyor from Kingston (Jamaica), to prevent her breaking up on the lee shore in the still adverse weather conditions, the vessel was scuttled. She was refloated in September and towed to Kingston where the cargo was discharged and temporary repairs undertaken. The shippers refused to have the cargo reloaded and she proceeded to New York in ballast for permanent repairs. A "No Cure, No Pay" salvage agreement had been put in place for a minimum of 33% of the salved value of the ship. The salvors claimed for $20,000 but this was reduced to $12,500 after arbitration. Both parties paid their own legal costs.

She was also involved in two interesting cases of jettison and the claiming of general average. Fourteen days out of Cadiz (Spain) with a cargo of salt for Newfoundland (Canada) she encountered a heavy SW gale. After five days of this the log reports that

"there was 15 inches (38 cm) of water in the hold and a quantity of salt had melted.(sic) Started pumps going."

The next entry reads

"Pumps found to be choked. Decks strained and leaking due to the constant working of the ship. 18 inches (46 cm) of water in the hold."

The decision was made to jettison part of the cargo to save the ship but in doing so the crew found it impossible to prevent the taking on of more water. For a fortnight more, with little time to celebrate Christmas, there was a constant battle to maintain the pumps which did not take kindly to having to evacuate a slurry of salt and water. On New Year's Day she was off the Cape Race light and signalled for a tug as there were by then only five of the crew fit to work ship due to injuries and frostbite.

"Blowing strongly from West. Intense frost. All standing rigging frozen. Ship labouring heavily and shipping large quantities of water."

reports the log. She arrived in St. John's nine days later.

Fifteen months later from the same port bound for Bahia (now Salvador, Brazil) with a cargo of codfish she is again in difficulties with her lee rail under water, leaking rivets in the engine room and pumps going continuously. It was discovered that the deck around the main mast was straining and leaking. A sail was rigged over the main hatch and jettison of the cargo commenced but of course in the bad weather even more water was shipped. Eventually she arrived in Bahia short of 578 drums and 1854 half-drums of codfish.

In both cases the partial sacrifice of the cargo had been undertaken to save the ship and remaining cargo. Both the hull and cargo interests contributed to the cost of the lost cargo, through their insurers of course.

MADELEINE CONSTANCE was certainly a lady of character and durability!

Claim: "All Is Not Lost"
Near the end of her passage from Tacoma (U.S.A.) to Falmouth (England) the barque ANDROMEDA (built 1890, 1928 g.r.t.) was swept onto rocks near the Lizard after dragging her anchors in a severe gale. At 04.30hrs on a dark February morning in 1915, with seas sweeping over the vessel, the master and crew took to the rigging. We hope that they all survived but their fate is not recorded in the claims book. It is noted that the ship was a total loss and that the underwriters paid £9,700.

A few months later it is recorded in some detail that all was not lost because some recoveries had been made, viz.

```
"Sundries washed ashore              £          17s- 10d
 Two chronometers saved              £   12-  0s-  0d
 Wreck sold                          £  208- 14s- 10d
 Less expenses                       £   28-  3s-  2d
 Recovered                           £  193-  9s-  5d "
```

The BMM records make no comment on the fate of the crew, although from Lloyd's List it is known the Portscatho rocket apparatus saved 27 including the captain's wife, 7 year old daughter and 15 year old sister-in-law. Sadly a New Zealand apprentice was washed overboard and lost.

Stranded and Refloated

There was undoubtedly a period of prosperity for British shipping in the immediate post-war years of 1919-20. Sadly it did not last and the world trade conditions that had applied from the turn of the century till 1912 re-established themselves.

It has been estimated that in 1908 two million tons of world shipping, half of which was British, was laid up. World trade had grown by 60% between 1900 and 1914 but the carrying capacity of the world's fleets had increased by 70%. The index of earnings per ton for British shipping in 1911/14 varied between 45% and 70% of its 1900 value. The United Kingdom had an imbalance in her trade with the rest of the world as exports outstripped imports (changed days!) and her ships returned home in ballast or at low freight rates. Little wonder then that losses were made.

British Marine's membership was not immune from these trends and when the post-war boom collapsed many laid up their tonnage or sold out. Some had of course not re-invested the proceeds from their wartime losses and during the 1920's had no incentive to do so. Also during the War there had been a deliberate policy to divert commodities away from coastal shipping to inland routes and it was difficult to recover these after four years. It is a measure of the decline in this sector that in 1913 coastal departures had amounted to 22 million net tons and in 1926 the figure was only 12 million tons even after the Government had introduced a subsidy to assist the coasters in the recovery of their trade. The effect was quite dramatic on the number of ships entered in Class 1, the British Iron, as this club drew the bulk of its entries from the coastal trade.

The situation had become so bad in 1922 that the management of the Association recommended that Class 1 be put into run-off, or as the minutes recorded it:

> " - in consequence of the depression in Shipping a large number of vessels are laid up or unemployed it is expedient to refrain from issuing any fresh policies on Hull, Materials and Machinery for the new year beginning 20th February 1922 during the period of such depression."

As is shown in Appendix I the premium income for Class 1 had fallen from £17,000 in 1909 to £2,800 in 1921 and the class was clearly not viable at this level. The committee continued to sit to supervise the run-off of outstanding claims from previous years. The Class was formally closed by a special resolution passed by the members in May 1925, " - the object and purpose of such class having been fulfilled and carried out - ". A return of premiums at a rate of £0.5% was made to those members entered at February 1922. The committee received £50 each in compensation for loss of office and the managers, who had no income by way of commission for three years yet had expenses of administration to pay, were granted £100 for their trouble. It is not without significance, in view of future events, that, to quote the Class minutes again, " - the affairs of the Class to be left in the hands of the Managers to close."

From that point onwards British Marine became, like so many others, an insurer mainly of P.&.I., Freight, Collision and War Risks. Those owners that remained in the British coastal trades took their hull and machinery insurance needs to the Lloyd's market. That is where they remained throughout the depressed 1920's and for twenty years beyond the end of World War 2. But, because of events that promote an eerie sense of déjà-vu in a commentator today, the late 1960's found the Lloyd's market experiencing difficulties with losses in underwriting and seeking to increase its rates to compensate. Lloyd's Joint Hull Formula and the Institute Time Clauses were revised in 1969 as a result of a sustained period of losses. The last profitable year on hull accounts had been 1962 by most reckonings and arguments were put forward for increases in rates of 25% for the 1970 year. Heavier penalties were sought for singleton vessels and small fleets in general as they were judged to have benefited disproportionately from the effects that international competition had on softening rates.

The coastal shipowners in the U.K. felt most uncomfortable with this and in taking stock of their position were soon harking back to their mutual traditions. The possibility of re-opening British Marine's hull class was discussed at a Board meeting in 1969 as a result of requests "from several members".

When Class 1 (Hull and Machinery) was refloated in 1971 the MORAY FIRTH (built 1960) was the first ship entered. She was owned by G.T. Gillie and Blair Ltd. of Newcastle (England), a company which has supplied two directors to British Marine, G.T. Gillie and J.T. Gillie, father and son, who served for a consecutive period of seventy-one years until 1989.

An extract from the Class 1 Entry book showing the details of MORAY FIRTH. In the top right hand corner it carries the number 71/001 designating her as the first entry in the new class.

YEAR ENDING *N 20 Feb.*   1972. 71/001

VESSEL 1 *Moray Firth IV*   MORTGAGEES
OWNER *The Firth shipping Co. Ltd.*

Attaching Date	Date Built	G.R.T.	Contributing Tonnage	H & M Value	T L Rate	Initial Call	Entry Fee	T L Premium £	p	Claims Paid £	p	Outstanding Claims £	p	Loss Ratio	Adjusted Tonnage
7/7/71	1960	612.89	920	£80.000 £60.000 is event of T2.	.6875%	+luk £2170 £463 £2432	6613	412 luk 49 £462	50 22 22						

The British Marine Mutual Insurance Association, Limited.

The Metropolitan Marine Mutual Insurance Association, Limited.

TELEGRAPHIC ADDRESS
"MUTUAL STOCK, LONDON"
TELEPHONE No.
AVENUE 5535

MANAGERS:

E. R. EVANS & CO.

H. J. BOXSIUS,
V. W. EVANS

12, LIME STREET,

LONDON, 6th November, 1925.
E.C. 3

Dear Sir(s),

We herewith have pleasure in enclosing Prospectus of the above British Marine Mutual Insurance Association, Ltd., which gives a synopsis of the various risks covered by each Class:—

Class II.—Protection and Indemnity.
Class III. Freight, Demurrage and Defence.
Class IV.—Collision (R.D.C.).
Class V.—War Risks.

This Association was established in 1869, and the Committee of each Class is composed of Owners of Coasting Tonnage, the number of vessels now on risk totalling about 750. Steamers contribute to calls on their actual gross tonnage, with a minimum of 150 tons, but where this exceeds 1,000 tons, a considerable reduction on the calls is made. Unlike other Associations, all Protection Claims are paid in full. In Class II., the average cost for the past three years has been 4/6 per ton, and in Class III., has not exceeded £5.5.0 per vessel per annum. Class IV., which covers the three-fourths of damage done to any other ship or vessel, has averaged 50/-% for the past three years, and in Class V., there has been no call since the Armistice.

As you will shortly be arranging your Insurances for the New Year, we trust that you will carefully consider the advantages given by this Association, and favour us with your support at the 20th February next.

Should you require any further information, we shall be pleased to write you again.

Yours faithfully,

E. R. Evans & Co.
Managers.

Enc.

This circular is what passed for aggressive selling in 1925. Virtue is made of the fact that no call had been made in Class V and that protection claims are paid in full "--- unlike other Associations --- ". Here we have Edward Evans' son, Victor, putting his name to a document that states that the Association dates from 1869. May we safely assume that he learned from his father when he went into the marine insurance business? There would seem to be more evidence for this date than for 1866 which has sometimes been quoted.

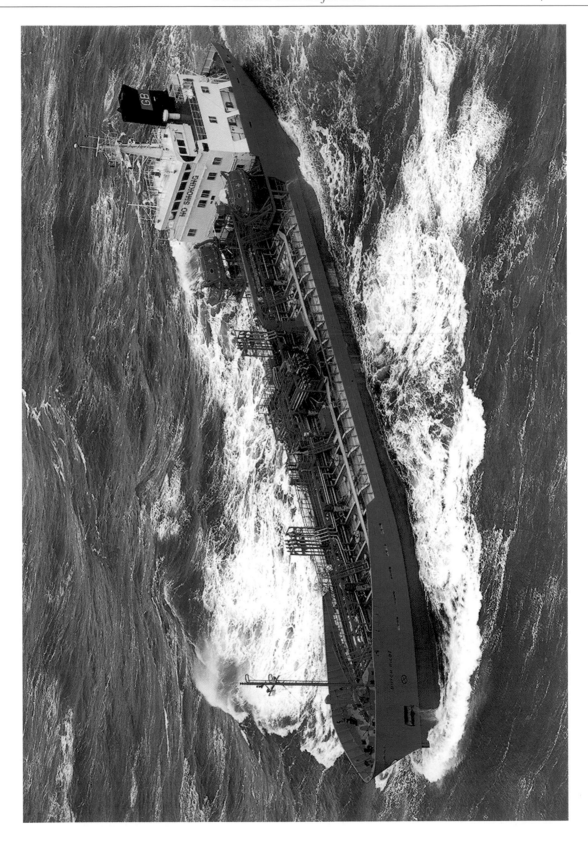

The Dutch company of Gebr. Broere BV have been members since 1971. Here we see a range of their vessels, old and new, that have been entered over these years. CORRIE BROERE (2527 g.r.t.) illustrates the shape of the coastal chemical tanker of the 1970's in contrast to the DUTCH PILOT, which was built in 1993 with stainless steel lined tanks (she is slightly smaller at 2137 g.r.t.). These tankers ply their trade in the North Sea, the Baltic and the Mediterranean but equally important to the company is their inland barge trade. Tankers like the 2170 d.w.t. DORDRECHT 35 are to be found on the Rhine, the Rhone and the Danube as well as in the canals of her native Holland.

It is important not to minimise what was involved in refloating the mutual concept. It was not simply a matter of putting up an 'open for business' sign and welcoming all-comers who had a cheque in their hands to pay for premiums. The unregulated days of a century before had gone, quite rightly, and now Government departments took a close interest in anyone who wanted to sell insurance to the public, even if that public was as sophisticated as the average British shipowner. How easy would it be to satisfy the authorities that British Marine was a fit and proper provider of a form of insurance that it had not practiced for over forty years? If approval was a long time in coming the commercial opportunity would be lost. What rates were to be charged? Well that was easy: "Lower than Lloyd's". What was the minimum number of entries to spread the risk in a viable book of business? Would the Lloyd's market co-operate in providing the necessary risk-spreading re-insurance, for total losses for example? How was the start to be financed and how many staff would be required to handle the inevitable claims efficiently? The British Marine's Management was directed to find the answers to these questions.

It was discovered that the old British Iron Club still qualified to offer mutual insurance. The 1925 Management had faithfully followed its instructions to run-off the book of business but it had not taken the ultimate step of obtaining a death certificate and arranging an honourable funeral. The British Iron was merely dormant and the hibernation was soon to end. If 1923 had been Winter then 1970 was Spring.

With this legal hurdle surmounted the practicalities could be considered. The minimum number of entries was set at two hundred ships. Brokers, not without some difficulty, provisionally organised particular average and total loss re-insurance cover. The National Westminster Bank agreed to provide an overdraft to support the cash flow in the start-up period. A prospectus was prepared and sent to existing and potential members.

At an Extraordinary General Meeting on 18th March 1970 it was agreed by the members that Class 1 should be revived. With that decision British Marine Mutual became what it remains to this day, the only London Club able to offer its members hull and machinery insurance on a mutual basis. (Others started up but did not survive.)

No date for the reflotation was set at that March meeting as some formidable problems still had to be overcome. The timing of the prospectus and the E.G.M. were both too late to influence members to change their insurer for the year that was to start on the traditional date of 20th February 1970 and by September the number of ships undertaking to join the revived club was short of the targeted two hundred. One hundred and thirteen ships, of which fifty-three were from nine German members, had decided to enter. In addition seven British companies, one Danish and one Dutch owner had pledged support. Efforts to attract more possible entries were made but persuading the shipowner to change at all, never mind in mid-year, was never going to be a simple matter. As 1971 approached it was felt that if the class was not opened soon the opportunity would be lost. A

Board meeting was not scheduled and the Directors, after consulting each other by telephone, took the courageous, and in retrospect justified, decision to authorise the Management to begin hull and machinery underwriting on New Year's Day, 1971.

Significant entrants in that first year were Peter Dohle of Hamburg with twenty-two ships and British Dredging with sixteen. Others who joined in those early days and whose names are still listed in the membership, or were to be so for many years, were W. Bruns of Hamburg (now Thien and Heyenga), Kelly's of Belfast, Ramsey Steamship of the Isle of Man, Crescent Shipping (a long-time member in Class 2 under its original name of London and Rochester), Offshore Marine and from Holland, Broere. These companies were to be among British Marine's longest and most loyal supporters of the mutual concept. Peter Dohle was to have two other notable firsts. He became the only non-British Director of the Association in March 1972 and less happily, in July 1971 his vessel, ALICIA (built 1970, 999 g.r.t.), became the initial claim on the new Class!

The re-insurance programme purchased for that first year was probably over-cautious and it certainly was relatively expensive. Excess of loss layers were purchased from the Lloyd's market which gave a cover of up to £1,000,000 and this was later increased to £2,000,000 in 1973/74. Total loss cover was at the members' expiring rates. Since the excess of loss re-insurance had minimum premium rates it became relatively less expensive to buy the greater the number of ships that were entered. The cost to the Class was going to level out as it grew in size and it was important to achieve this critical mass.

The new class went into its second year in February 1972 with over two hundred ships entered. This was encouraging, but the first fourteen months' underwriting results were less so. The cost of claims, re-insurance and administration had come to nearly £700,000 and this necessitated a supplementary call on the members of £225,000 or 47% of the initial call. A

BALTIMAR VENUS is a 2,700 d.w.t. multi-purpose vessel owned by Baltimar Shipping Aps. of Vedbaek, Denmark, and trades world-wide.

Two views of the modern container ship. The loaded 5340 g.r.t. LILIENTHAL (above) is one of the larger ships entered in British Marine for Class 1, 2 and 3 cover and has a container capacity of 580 TEU. Built in 1994, thirteen years later, the FRONTIER AMERICA (opposite) is strengthened for heavy cargo and can achieve a speed of 16 knots from her 4,800 H.P. engine. Both are operated by Thien and Heyenga of Hamburg, who through their antecedents have been members since 1971. Their m.t. KEITUM (below) of 1988 is a 4,900 d.w.t. oil/chemical tanker and typical of the high quality German membership of the Association, being double-hulled.

supplementary had been anticipated, it always was in those days, and while it was a stiff one neither the Directors nor the membership was sufficiently discouraged to contemplate doing anything else but press ahead with the re-formed class. The 1973/74 year's supplementary was even higher at 70% and this gave pause for thought and reconsideration of the advisability of proceeding beyond February 1974. The Board's collective nerve held and the outcome of their debate in September 1973 was that the Class should remain open for the 1974/75 year. Board resolutions were all very well but they were no more than an expression of intent if the membership did not give its support by renewing. They did and from then on the affairs of the Class prospered. Clearly, supplementary calls or not, the costs must have been attractive relative to those of the 'opposition'. No doubt the 'no profit in the rates' aspect of the mutual association also had its attractions.

The prospects were beginning to look quite bright but for one problem that had its origins in the rules of the old British Iron Club. These rules were adopted as the basis for the restart, understandably, but they had been drafted in 1876 at the time of the incorporation and had not changed in principle before the class went

ATLANTIC LADY, a 'hatchless' container ship of the Oost Atlantic Lijn BV.

into lay-up in 1922.

However much had changed in the business of shipping. The class was no longer based mainly on a membership in which one type of ship, the British coaster for example, was dominant. The Board, in reviewing the operation of the Class for that first 1971/72 year and in particular the "Final Call" (their capitals), concluded that "the operation of Rule 7 produces anomalies and is inequitable".

Rule 7 embodied the purest spirit of 19th century mutuality. The call system operated like this. Under the original rules every ship in Class 1 paid a relatively small advance or first call. In a sense it was a sort of deposit or down payment for the real call which was expected when all the claims were in. The supplementary call when it inevitably came was the multiple of the claims incurred by each ship. A ship with no claims paid no supplementary call. A vessel with a big claim paid a big supplementary call. Hence the money required to balance the Class books in any one year came mostly from a relatively small number of ships which had suffered large claims. It was optimistically assumed that on the swings and roundabouts of the shipping business everything would be smoothed out over a number of years. However serious cash flow problems were created in some companies by this approach with the attendant danger that some shipowners would fall off the roundabout before they had the opportunity to climb aboard the swing. The final indignity was that this draconian rule applied even to a member who had a credit balance, i.e. when his premiums exceed the costs of his claims in the year in question!

So strongly was this principle of 'sameness' adhered to that members' requests for unusual extensions to their cover were often refused. The basis for the refusal was that since no one else was running the risk in question it was considered not to be mutual. As late as 1972 a request to be insured "to embrace the risks consequent on the towage of ice-bergs" was refused because of "the non-mutuality inherent in such operations". An unusual request certainly but not one for which it was unable to devise a rate, even one prohibitively discouraging. The reason for the refusal was not that the operation was too dangerous, but that nobody else was doing it. Presumably if the demand for fresh water in hot and arid parts of the world had made the towing of icebergs commonplace a British Mutual Ice Club would have been quite happily incorporated.

Such fundamentalism could not long survive if the Club was to become truly international with a membership which would want to conduct its affairs in many different trades and geographic areas. Victorian simplicity was abandoned in favour of 20th century sophistication. The members in Annual General Meeting changed the rules so that a member's past claims record was taken into account in setting his premium. In this way he was judged against the average underwriting cost of the membership as a whole, a much fairer system.

This important change came into effect for the 1974/75 year and it could be said that from that point on the Class was truly refloated and in the fairway. The development and growth of the Class in the last twenty years is illustrated in

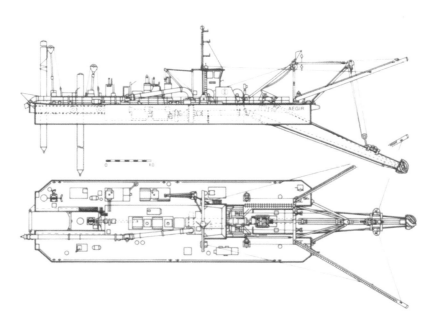

Ballast Nedam Dredging of Zeist in Holland operate dredgers on a world-wide basis and enter their vessels in British Marine. This drawing of their cutter suction dredger AEGIR illustrates the layout and mechanisms of what many regard as mystery ships.

Appendix II. In 1996 there were over two thousand five hundred vessels entered and the premium income was £50,000,000. Even when the effects of inflation are taken into account this represents real growth. What was a speculative venture twenty years ago is now the largest class in the Association in terms of premium income and is among the top three hull books written in the City of London.

Today a supplementary call in this Class is unknown. It remains a mutual club with a second call on the members a theoretical possibility, but the theory has not been tested since those early days. Today's underwriting skills combined with a sound re-insurance programme and not least the quality of the management of the membership who enter their vessels make sure of that.

Claim: "British Marine does not do Thing by Halves"

In 1973 the owners of mv AROSIA (built 1969, 3251g.r.t.) decided to lengthen her and subsequently put her into drydock in Hamburg to have the work carried out. British Marine was informed as a matter of course and indicated that new terms would be offered after the reconstruction was completed. Apparently due to negligence on the part of the drydock personnel when the vessel was in two parts, the after section fell over against the dock wall and was damaged. The owners sought to have the cost of the repair paid on account by the Club.

However British Marine was advised by its lawyers, Admiralty Court solicitors, that at the time of the accident the vessel had ceased to be an entity and was no longer the "subject matter of a hull policy." On this basis the claim had to be repudiated. Not altogether surprisingly the owners fielded equally learned legal opinion that took the opposite view, i.e. that two halves did in law make a whole.

The board was quite divided on what to do: split in two in fact. The dispute was a narrow one, all rested on the interpretation of the wording of the policy. The possibility of going to arbitration was considered but no Judgement of Solomon was needed here. What precedents would be set by a decision that the two halves were covered by one policy? How was the hull value to be apportioned between the fore and after sections? If the after half became a constructive total loss what then would be the fate of the bow section? If the dockyard sued for wreck removal need the Club only pay to have the stern removed?

An amicable settlement was clearly what was needed and Management was sent off to negotiate one. Naturally when the owner asked for 100% of the cost of the repairs British Marine offered half.

Tugs

Throughout its existence tug owners have entered their vessels in the British Marine. As the following sequence of photographs, drawn from member's sources, shows they have been in the Club since the days of the steam driven paddler in the late 19th century until the cycloidal and azimuthal propelled craft of the 1990's. In many ways they typify the small specialised ship that was attracted to British Marine and on which it built its reputation as a provider of tailor made insurance knowledge and claims service.

ADMIRAL, owned by Steele and Bennie of Glasgow, was an iron hulled paddle steamer (a single 36^1/$_2$ inch cylinder, delivered 50 H.P.) built in 1886.

Although built thirteen years earlier than ADMIRAL, CHALLENGER had almost double the horsepower from her two single cylinder side lever engines and is an elegant example of the twin-funnelled tugs of the period. Such craft sometimes had independent control of each paddle and were highly manoeuvrable long before twin screws or azimuthal or cycloidal systems appeared !

By 1914 *when United Towing built the HULLMAN paddles had been replaced by the screw and this tug's 650 H.P. was produced by a triple expansion steam engine.*

The FORAGER *of Steele and Bennie was an example of the transitional tug of the 1940's. She was still steam propelled but she was oil and not coal fired. With an overall length of around 100 feet she was no longer than ADMIRAL and CHALLENGER and many harbour tugs were of similar size.*

*Not all members limited themselves to harbour and estuary towing.
FOREMAN (1959) was United Towing's first sea-going motor tug. This Hull
(England) company was well established in coastal and deep sea towage and
this tug's 1000 B.H.P was the most powerful they had built to that time.*

*LLOYDSMAN was probably United Towing's most famous tug after her
exploits on Fisheries Protection duties. Built in 1971 she had ten times the
horsepower of the FOREMAN and shows how much the demands of the
market had changed in a decade.*

SALVAGEMAN, of 1980, here seen towing a jack up rig, was the most powerful tug that United towing built at 11280 B.H.P.

Clyde Shipping Co. Ltd's FLYING PHANTOM *was developed, as were many others in the towage industry, to meet the oil companies' demands for firefighting capabilities during and after tanker berthing. Built in 1985 the top hydrant was 70 feet (21 metres) above the waterline.*

With the LADY MOIRA we are back to harbour towage on the Humber. This 1977 example of United Towing's design thinking is still approximately 100 feet overall but her horsepower is 2900 B.H.P and she has twin screws.

A variation on the twin screw harbour tug, Tees Towing's YARM CROSS (1979), was fitted with twin rudder propellers of the Schottel type. Stylistically and technically different from the LADY MOIRA she had much the same pulling power.

In comparison FIERY CROSS (1993) shows the very latest thinking in the design of the firefighting harbour tug. She is seen here in the livery of Cory Ship Towage Ltd., who acquired the Tees company, and is a 1700 B.H.P Voith Schneider driven tractor tug. She is rather different from the ADMIRAL!

In recent years important European tug owners have become members of British Marine and the ZEEBRUGGE (1992) of Union de Remorquage et Sauvetage of Antwerp, is an example of this modern tonnage. There are similarities between her and BUGSIER 16, also built in 1992, and indeed with the FIERY CROSS, that indicate that from quite different traditions the modern tug has evolved to much the same point.

In June 1993 m.t. BRITISH TRENT caught fire after a collision off the Belgian coast and was attended by the firefighting tugs of British Marine member Union de Remorquage et Sauvetage of Antwerp.

Under New Management

A quarter of a century after the incorporation of British Marine as a company limited by guarantee we find that Edward Evans was still at the helm but he had introduced his son Victor, a man in his early thirties, into the partnership to work alongside himself. Victor, the second son, who had trained as an engineer, came into the business after the first son Reginald had declined to do so. Also there was his colleague, Walter Stocken, who incidentally was to become Victor's brother-in-law. Stocken had extensive contacts in sailing barge companies in Devon and Kent.

The firm of W. W. Stocken acted as the Association's solicitor and there are regular references to his legal firm in the disbursement records and even to fees being outstanding to him. Edward Evans died in December 1901 and it was found that his will had not made adequate provision for the continuation of the company, a remarkable state of affairs as it was among his principal assets. It was arranged with his widow that the company was to be run by Victor Evans and his principal clerk, Henry J.P. Boxsius, who at that time was by far the more experienced in insurance of the two. In later years Boxsius was to earn himself a formidable reputation as an expert on the legal aspects of marine insurance. A few years later a dispute arose as to the interpretation of the agreement between Mrs Evans and Boxsius and Victor Evans and possibly as a result of this, Stocken, who acted as her adviser, left the Association in 1903. He took with him some of the barge business and formed the Sailing Ships Mutual. Subsequently Stocken with his marine mutual experience and his marine business contacts went on to establish himself, three years later, as the manager of the association that was to become the Steamship Mutual. It is today one of the major P.&.I. clubs in world shipping.

This photograph was taken at the wedding of Victor William Evans (1875 - 1958) to Barbara Stocken. He followed his father Edward into the management of the British Marine in 1901.

Victor Evans and Harry Boxsius were to be in double harness for another forty seven years in charge of the affairs of British Marine. (From the distribution of the partnership's income between the two men there is no doubt that Boxsius was considered to be the senior partner.) They saw it through the trauma of two World Wars and the difficult times of the depression of the 1920's when British Marine's difficulties reflected those of British shipping in general. But for the continuance of the P.&.I. class in this period the Association and its Managers would have had a lean time after the closure of the Hull and Machinery class in 1925. The Managers certainly earned the plaudits of the members for their skilful negotiations with the Ministry of War Transport in World War 2 on the vital question of the total loss values under the War Risks policies.

Coe Metcalf Shipping Ltd. joined British Marine at the time of the amalgamation with the Short Sea Mutual and in the intervening period has moved away from its traditional dry cargo trades into more specialised businesses. For example PHOLAS (3775 g.r.t.) was converted for sea bed survey work. Built in 1978 the REDTHORN a 1600 g.r.t. dry cargo vessel, and the 1963 JOHN M, seen here punching her way through the Irish Sea, are typical of the earlier era.

But as the 1940's came to a close the premium income for the four extant classes was no greater in total than it had been thirty years before and there seemed to be an acceptance that this was the natural order. Little had changed in their methods of acquiring and recording business in that period. Their income, based as it was on the premium income of the Association, was quite modest by the standards of the time. Boxsius was an octogenarian and Evans nearly so and it would have been surprising if they were not resting on their laurels so to speak. (Evans died in 1958 aged eighty-three and Boxsius a year later in his ninety-fourth year.) But what was most disturbing of all to the committee members, all of whom were considerably younger than the managing partners, was that there had been no succession planned to take over the affairs of the Association by youthful but appropriately experienced men. In May 1952 the committee resolved to appoint a sub-committee to discuss, inter alia, the current position of the Club and its prospects and to make recommendations as to its future.

The sub-committee's findings were disturbing and its solution quite radical. It openly expressed its concern at the lack of management succession and saw the preponderance of British coastal and estuarial ships of under 2,000 g.r.t. (80% of the total) in the membership as leaving the Club exposed to a narrow market sector. It concluded that vigorous action was needed to attract new tonnage and that an overhaul of the constitution of the Association and its relationship with its Managers was essential. The sub-committee members were unanimously of the opinion that the Club should be continued as a separate entity despite the difficulties it was certainly facing. Full consultation with the Management had taken place throughout the process and the two grand old men were realistic enough to understand and accept that change was inevitable.

The main proposal was that the agreement with E.R. Evans and Company, enshrined in the 1876 incorporation documents, should be terminated and that in future the affairs of the Association should be conducted by managers who were

---

Claim: "A Hostage to Ill Fortune"

A small ship ran aground in the Caribbean. She was carrying about 20 tons of bunkers and the Captain of the Port demanded a very large sum of money to cover the possibility of oil pollution. British Marine assured the Captain that there would be no danger to his shoreline and paid for a tug, barge and pump to remove all the offending liquid. A message was received however that the large sum of money was still required.

A passing hurricane took the wreck well out to sea and all danger to the Port's environment was permanently removed. A relieved British Marine sent a pleasant message congratulating all concerned on their mutual good luck. A reply was received however that a sum of money, of slightly lower quantum, was still required. This request was declined and the Association was led to believe that it would regret its obstinacy. The file was closed.

A month later a containership, entered in the British Marine, berthed in the same republic and was boarded by armed troops who informed her master that his P.&.I. club would explain why his ship was being arrested. The Captain of the Port was unconcerned about such refinements as different ownership and indicated that the Association knew what he wanted.

The moral dilemma of British Marine's Board and staff was considerable. Business ethics gave a clear, if academic, answer to the problem but how do you evaluate the cost of detention of an innocent vessel and the stress to her crew in such a situation?

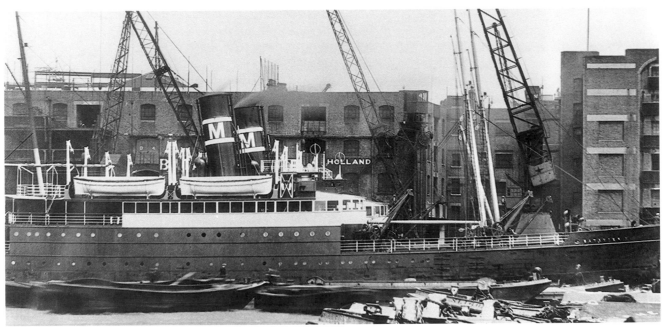

Two Muller ships in the Pool of London in the 1930s.

BATAVIER V (Wm. Muller and Co. NV.) traded from Rotterdam (Holland) to London with general and reefer cargo in the 1960's (she was built in 1959). One of the members' ships on which the then General Manager, Captain Edward Evans, was known to have taken a 'vacation'. (F. Leeman)

directly employed by the Club and supervised, not by committees, but by a Board of Directors. These managers would be salaried and not commission earning. We are used to this arrangement in British Marine today and it is not easy to imagine what a revolutionary idea this was in 1952. It flew in the face of three-quarters of a century of tradition within British Marine and was quite contrary to the practice in other London clubs, most of whom were then as they are still today, run by independently owned management companies and partnerships. The sub-committee however had looked to the different model at that time operating in the North of England P.&.I. Club and decided to adopt its principle of a directly employed management. Apart from the stimulus that the change itself would provide to the forward movement of the Club it eliminated the final profit margin from the Club's costs, i.e. the management commission on premiums paid. It was a return to one of the basic principles of the 18th century mutuals.

It was accepted that Boxsius would retire in February 1953 and Evans would follow him one year later. Compensation terms were agreed with both of these old servants of the Association. The pain of the separation, if there was such, was eased for Victor Evans in a proposal, emanating from a committee member, that his son, Captain Edward W. Evans, "was the man for the job"; the job being that of understudying him for the last year of his time in office with the objective of taking over from him. In fact he was to share the managing of the revival of the Association with another, F.M. Vaughan.

New Articles and a new Memorandum of Association were drawn up and were accepted by the members at an Extraordinary General Meeting in November 1954. The Chairman of the new Association was Christopher S. Rowbotham, a shipowner and Lloyd's broker, and the Vice-Chairman Cecil Crosthwaite, a tugowner from the North-east of England. Both had been active members of the sub-committee that had promoted the change. The new era dawned on February 20th the next year. The young lions on the new Board of Directors could change much but even they could not change the date on which the Baltic became free of ice!

It is from this date that the modern British Marine originated. The Association was to be run by shipowners for shipowners in the most direct manner from this time onward. The burden of success or failure was accepted by the type of businessmen who were used to making that kind of decision daily but with the significant difference that they answered to their peers. The other "shareholders" were shipowners too. It is a sobering thought for any British Marine Director to have to account for an increase in operating expenses, for example, at an Annual Meeting composed entirely of cost conscious fellow owners. He takes comfort in the thought that if the roles were reversed he would be equally unforgiving.

Edward Walter Evans (1907 - 1974) became the first General Manager of British Marine after the reorganisation of the management structure in 1953 and continued the tradition of Evans family service to the Association until it was three generations and nearly a century old.

Two new managers were recruited in January 1953, the aforesaid Captain Edward Evans and Martin Vaughan. Evans was to oversee British matters and Vaughan was to seek out the new non-British tonnage that it had been decided must be brought into the Club to halt the decline in membership. Both were to learn all they could from Victor Evans.

Edward Evans, then in his forties, was a master mariner who had captained ships of the United Molasses fleet and had risen to be commodore of the Kelly fleet operating out of Belfast. He was widely respected in British coastal shipping circles and combined considerable insurance experience with that of the practical

Tropical Shipping and Construction Co. Ltd's TROPIC TIDE of 1993 is entered for P.&I. and spends her time trading from Florida (U.S.A.) to the Caribbean with containers.

seaman. (Irked at being desk-bound he was famous for spending his vacations on delivery voyages of members' ships.) For the next twenty years his was to be the name most readily associated with that of British Marine in the minds of the U.K. membership.

Martin Vaughan came to British Marine with previous P.&.I. experience and was well versed in re-insurance matters. He spoke German fluently and his secretary was German and they were the spearhead of the Club's attack on the European market. With the support and encouragement of the Board he developed contacts in Germany, Scandinavia and the Low Countries. Through his relationship with Herr Scheffer of Carl Rehder he first built the association with the Hamburg brokerage firm that was to become Hubertus Clausius and one of British Marine's enduring and most productive relationships.

The two men, though very different in temperament and style (Vaughan had a legal turn of mind and did not spend his holidays on the quarterdeck), increased and stabilised the Association's membership, as is discussed elsewhere. They worked in complement to each other and tended their respective geographic gardens until 1965 when Vaughan retired. It had been one of the most productive decades in the Club's history, one during which the tonnage entered in Class 2 had increased by 14%, and had ensured its survival.

For another eight years and into his seventh decade Evans ran the show single-handed. Remembering the hard lesson that they had learned from the Boxsius example about planning for succession, the Directors began the process of looking for the next generation of management. In 1974 they brought in John de L. Lewis to act as understudy and to absorb the ethos and methods of the business. Sadly his apprenticeship was all too short for Captain Evans died suddenly two months later just as the Club was about to be plunged into another period of change.

Lewis was no greenhorn in the problems of marine insurance having had the salutary experience of seeing the demise of the Oceanus Club at first hand. Lewis had an Extra Master's qualification and had whiled away his time at sea between watches by taking a legal degree and had been called to the bar as a member of Gray's Inn in 1966. His time at sea had been with the New Zealand Shipping Company and Canadian Pacific. While more than a little useful to the work of the Association, Lewis's seagoing experience inclined him to yachting rather than entered vessels in his leisure time. Walking was also a preferred holiday pastime and it was sometimes difficult, but not impossible, to communicate with the General Manager when he was off in the Himalayas. He worked closely with the Directors for a remarkably constructive period of twenty years during which there were to be take-overs, an unusual activity in the placid world of mutual insurance, a move off-shore and significant changes in the international composition of the Association.

As British Marine entered the 1990's Lewis took the initiative of suggesting to the Board that he should make way for a younger man to take the helm in what he judged would be another time of rapid development. He had seen that more and more time was being taken up, not so much on the still important service of claims procedures, but equally on the more complex involvement in the financial and legal aspects of a truly international business. Under him British Marine had climbed to a higher plateau and the vistas of even higher ground ahead that could be reached should be the objective set to a new General Manager. And so Richard D. Leslie was appointed Deputy General Manager in August 1992.

Leslie, an economist by training, came with insurance and investment experience and a background in international operations in offshore and oil industry servicing principally with Christian Salvesen Group, the long-established Scottish business and one-time shipping conglomerate. Not a sailor, his walking tended to involve following golf balls and his interest in vintage cars is an antidote to days spent on marine matters. Gradually he replaced Lewis in the decision making process and in November 1993 he assumed the full responsibility of accounting to the Board for the affairs of British Marine. The latest ascent has begun well with a strengthened and remotivated team.

The three employee-managers whose service has spanned the forty years since the arrangement with E.R. Evans and Company was determined have brought different management styles, as befitted their differing personalities, to the affairs of British Marine. All in turn absorbed its distinctive shipowner culture. The combination of the man and the organisation blended to respond to the challenge of the time and to take British Marine forward. In 1996 it is still moving forward.

Claim: "When is a 'Claim' Not a Claim?"

Human nature being what it is there may be a tendency for owners to exaggerate ever so slightly the cost of the repairs when an insurance recovery is involved. However the insurer's surveyors are alive to such frailties and they and the loss adjusters see to it that a balance fair to all is struck. Thus fraud, for that is what it is, is all but eliminated.

In one case however the system did not work. An odd claims pattern had developed in the case of one owner and one particular repair yard featured in all of them. The attention of the Association's surveyors was directed to this interesting relationship.

Under pressure of stringent examination of the size of a bill, the repair yard manager broke down and asked the Association to protect him from the pressure he was receiving from the shipowner's manager. The threat to the work hungry yard was that unless bills were issued for the "right" amounts they would not be paid. He knew that British Marine would pay fair costs but he was becoming afraid of the demands placed on him. The sad history was disclosed to the Association's solicitor and a report was prepared for the British Marine Board and for the shipowner himself. There was no suggestion that the owner personally had been involved in the fraud.

The moral of the tale are that the high professional behaviour of the surveyor contributed to the discovery of the fraud as did the pressure that the greed of the fraudster put on the unwilling participant. The most fundamental rule of mutuality had been broken. The Board of Directors took the straightforward view that however innocent the owner was personally his entry in the Association must be terminated immediately and so it was.

The Non-British Marine

From its inception British Marine was not exclusively British in its membership. The 1876 class rules reflected what was the practice of the day before the formality of the incorporation. Provision was made for non-British entries if they conformed to the standards of a recognised Classification Society. The original hull classes, Nos. 4 and 5, British A1 and British Marine Mutual, admitted American ships which were given seven years by Lloyd's Register of Shipping at their first classification as were ships "3/3rds in Veritas for not less than seven years; or any other classification equal to the above."

Many took advantage of these rules and in particular the French sailing fleet was well represented. (British Marine was not unique among the London clubs in insuring these ships.) In the late 19th and early 20th centuries the French sailing fleet was modern and of high quality. It was supported by its Government to sustain a French monopoly of their own coastal and colonial traffic. The policy had the effect of prolonging the use of sail by the French at a time when they might otherwise have moved to steam. The vessels came to be regarded as welcome mutual members, gradually overcoming the chauvinism of adverse rating conditions they were given in the early days of their entry. Throughout the shipping depression, prior to the 1914-18 War, the French sailing ships were financially secure and well able, thanks to their subsidies, to meet their mutual call obligations.

With the closure of the British Marine hull classes in the 1920's, however, the membership became concentrated almost entirely in the United Kingdom. After all the Protection and Indemnity classes had grown up principally to meet the demands of new British legislation in the rapidly changing social climate of the last decades of the 19th century and non-British shipowners did not always relate to the types of risks that such new laws brought. While this might have been a valid explanation to begin with, there is no doubt that the doldrums into which British Marine sailed in the inter-war period left it unresponsive to changes in the international marine insurance market. As we have seen previously Class 2 stagnated for nearly twenty years. Other London based P.&.I. clubs were able to attract overseas entrants during this same era.

It was not until after the rejuvenation brought about by the 1953 move to restructure the management of the Association that there was a drive to increase the membership by attracting continental European shipowners to join. A target of 25% of the tonnage in each class was set for the Management. The entry of vessels over 2000 g.r.t. was to be encouraged. (An upper limit was later to be set at 5,000 tons.) Vaughan was sent off to the Netherlands, Germany, Copenhagen and Stockholm to persuade shipowners there of the benefits of the Club's services.

Through the agency of Herr Bruns of Hamburg seven German ships entered in May 1954 and in February 1955 nineteen Dutch vessels from the fleet of W. H. Muller and Company became fixed premium members. By January 1958 a dinner was being held in Hamburg, attended by twenty-two representatives of German owners, to celebrate the entry of the 100th German ship. Incidentally, it was in Hamburg in 1965 that the Board began the tradition, now well-established, of meeting at least once a year in a port outside the United Kingdom. Adventurously, the Directors had met for the only time in ninety years outside London, in the wilds of Glasgow in 1957. Perhaps this ought to qualify as their first truly 'foreign' expedition. Appendix III shows the rapid change in the composition of the Club in the 1950's. Non-British, and in particular the Dutch and German, entries grew to account for more than half of the ships and tonnage of the Association at a time when British membership was virtually static. (The data includes only those ships directly entered with the Association and not those re-insured, like the French fishing vessels which were taken on risk in the 1960's.)

British Marine was re-learning the lesson of supplying the market with its needs. It began to cover German officers for sickness and accident risks, the Fürsorgegesetz (for which the premiums were collected in Deutsche Marks), and this no doubt contributed to the growth of the German membership. Despite the

The twisted railway lines lie in the Severn mud as the result of the collision of the
WASTDALE H with one of the piers. (National Waterways Museum)

Claim: "A Tragedy on the Severn"
A collision between two oil barges in 1960 caused loss of life and severe damage to the rail link between England and Wales. The mv WASTDALE H (built 1951, 229 g.r.t.) ran into one of the piers of the railway bridge in fog and brought down two spans of the bridge. She then collided with the British Marine ship, the mv ARKENDALE H (built 1937, 229 g.r.t.). Both were carrying petroleum spirit and the subsequent explosion and fire cost the lives of five men. The main domestic gas supply line which the bridge also carried was fractured and many homes had their gas cut off as a safety precaution. The claims for loss of life were paid timeously and in full. The British Transport Commission sued for £0.5 million for property damage but the Club entered a defence of limitation of liability. The findings of a subsequent public enquiry allowed the limitation to be upheld. Based on the property limitation at that time a sum of £4422 was paid.

Red Funnel Group Ltd. (owned by Associated British Ports Ltd.) operates these two new car/passenger ferries RED FALCON and RED OSPREY (built 1994/5), between Southampton and the Isle of Wight (England). Serving a similar purpose, at a slightly higher speed, Condor Shipping Ltd's hydrofoil, CONDOR 7, runs from the Channel Islands to the French mainland.

John Kelly's
BALLYGRAINEY
(built 1983, 1599 g.r.t.)
represented the modern
face of this longtime
member of the
Association and contrasts
considerably with their
earlier entrants like
BALMARINO.

KILGAS CHAMPION, a
Class 1 entry of Knud I.
Larsen of Denmark, is a
1334 g.r.t. liquid gas
carrier and demonstrates
the range and variety of
modern tonnage insured
by British Marine.

Built in 1986, and
entered in Classes 1, 2
and 3, the HOO
FALCON is a good
example of R. Lapthorn
and Co. Ltd's
development of the
modern coaster.

competition from a newly established P.&.I. club, in that country British Marine built up relationships with the Guilds, e.g. the Rendsburg, a hull mutual, through which it secured business. It is worth noting that this period saw a growth in interest in P.&.I. in Germany, a type of insurance that many owners did not carry, with the start of new clubs and the entry of British Marine to the market.

At this time an agent, Herr Kurt Scheffer of Messrs. Carl Rehder, was appointed. He worked closely with Management (providing a good foil to Vaughan) for thirteen years to build up the German membership until his death in 1968 when the still continuing relationship with the Clausius family began. There is no doubt that the growth of the German membership has owed much to the firm of Hubertus Clausius from whose energy and commercial skills both the members and the Association have benefited. The agency became one of the largest producing brokerages in the British Marine and income from Germany has accounted for as much as 15% of the total of annual premiums.

WALENBURG (KNSM Kroonburgh B.V., 1967) was caught in ice in the Baltic en route for St. Petersburg but thankfully suffered no damage. (F. Leeman)

In parallel with this agencies were also established in Belgium (Langlois and Company) and in Holland (at various times Vinke and Company, De Vlaming and Van Ommeren) where Folkert Leemans became the Association's main channel of communications for many years. He had worked with W.H. Muller and Company, whose ships had joined the Association in 1955 as noted above, and although officially retired he was still acting for British Marine until 1992 operating through the courtesy of KNSM-Kroonburgh from their offices.

The new membership did bring its strains with it and British Marine had to learn to adjust its age-old methods of underwriting. In the post-1946 era, it had been a Club almost exclusively for British shipowners carrying bulk cargoes in ships of around 1000 g.r.t. In 1970 it included liquid and perishable cargo carriers (of up to 10,000 g.r.t.), many trading worldwide, salvage and harbour tugs, dredgers, and offshore supply vessels. In addition it was involved in re-insurance and time charter risks. The tradition of treating everyone as if they were in the same trade clearly no longer stood up to any serious examination.

The possibility of forming a separate Class 2 for non-British members was debated and quickly discarded. The same problem of mix of entries was to emerge when Class 1 got underway in its new form a few years later and the same solution had to be adopted for both Classes, i.e. individual rating of ships and owners depending on their claims record, the type of ship and the risks being run.

Until 1972 this growth came entirely from the P.&.I. classes and it did much to revive the fortunes of British Marine. There was to be another surge in non-British entries when the hull class was re-opened. The demand for the re-start had come mainly from British owners in the first instance but of course having dipped its toe into warmer continental P.&.I. waters and rather enjoyed the sensation, British Marine saw no reason to exclude Dutch, German and Scandinavian owners from the revived hull class. Indeed without them Class 1 would not have reached the critical mass which made the re-opening viable anything like as quickly as it did.

The full development of British Marine's international composition in the last twenty years is illustrated by the fact that today the percentage of total annual premium income from the U.K. is 30%. Apart from United Kingdom registered tonnage the main national groupings in the Hull and Machinery class, judged by the measure of premium income, are the Germans, the Dutch, the Danes, the Canadians and the Irish. The Germans again lead the field in Class 2 and they are closely followed by entries from Holland, Italy, Hong Kong, America, South Korea, Denmark, Norway and Australia. In the two main classes in 1996, there are numbered some twenty shipowning countries with major premium contributions. In total the national flags of over ninety nations fly on British Marine insured ships.

"Excess of a Million Pounds"

There was a time when re-insurance had been prohibited by the law of the United Kingdom. The 1876 Articles of Association of British Marine made it a proper activity for the members to engage in: "insurance includes re-insurance" they said. This had only been given clearance by the 1867 Inland Revenue Act. Before then it was illegal to re-insure any marine risk except where the original insurer had died or was insolvent. Any suggestion that an underwriter was not good for his own risks and was spreading them around to others was regarded with so much mistrust that it was proscribed. We presume that Edward Evans had taken advantage of the change in the law in the seven clubs that he managed and had the powers to engage in re-insurance written into the Articles at the time of the incorporation.

When we consider what an integral role re-insurance plays in protecting the members' interests today it is strange to contemplate such a state of affairs. Over the last one hundred and twenty years the Association has both sought extra cover from others and equally from time to time offered it to those who needed additional protection on their own account. Today we think of it almost entirely as the main activity in a strategy designed to guarantee the member freedom from the uncertainties of unlooked for and unwanted additional calls.

In the early days of the Association re-insurance took the elementary form of spreading the insured value of a vessel over several classes. The 1876 rules had limited the maximum entered value to £2,000 on any one bottom and it was quite usual to find a £6,000 hull spread across the British Iron, British A1 and other clubs outwith the British Marine group for £2,000 in each. In this way sudden fluctuations in calls due to the impact of claims of an exceptional nature were controlled to a degree by spreading the burden over a larger number of shipowners.

For P.&.I. cover, risk sharing was formalised in 1899 with the formation of a "mutual of mutuals", the London Group. This was essentially a pooling arrangement between the then six major British P.&.I. clubs. The object was to pool, i.e. share a proportion of a claim among all the members of the Group. In this way the catastrophic claim was met not entirely by the members of the Club in which it originated but partly by all the members of the other clubs in the pool. The club which was the primary insurer might take, say, the first £4,000 of a £6,000 claim and all would then contribute in agreed proportions to the remaining £2,000.

Subsequently the London Group expanded to become the International Group through the inclusion of Scandinavian, American and Japanese mutuals. British Marine, in common with many other smaller clubs in the late 19th century did not join this pool, but preferred, as it does today, to remain independent of the arrangement.

In 1951 the International Group extended this protection system by buying additional cover to top up its own pool. It purchased it from the proprietary markets in London and throughout the world and thus added a third layer of protection to the P.&.I. insurance for the shipowner. Literally hundreds of syndicates and insurance companies contribute to the provision of this cover. With the public aware fully of the costs of dealing with oil pollution from stranded ships, for example, the marine insurance industry has felt constrained to offer cover against the possibility of claims of hundreds of millions of U.S dollars. British Marine also purchases this particular type of "excess of loss" cover for its members from a number of reputable London, European, Bermudan and American re-insurers.

British Marine's re-insurance premiums run to millions of pounds today to secure cover of hundreds of millions and not much has changed since the turn of the century, only the number of zeros in the figures. Before the First World War

Coe Metcalf Shipping Ltd's bitumen carrier was built in 1964 and acquired secondhand by them. She was renamed GORDON THOMAS and as far as is known is the only vessel entered in British Marine that has been called after a Vice-Chairman of the Association. (G.W. Thomas was a director from 1978 until 1992). At the time of writing both he and his namesake are showing a similar durability although his year of launching predates that of the ship.

Class 2 could be re-insured with Lloyd's underwriters, excess of £5,000, for around £40. Ten years later the same protection cost £337. It takes a long time before the records show the order of premiums and cover that would be recognised as significant today. Of course the Association lost its hull classes in the 1920's and the remaining P.&.I. clubs stagnated for the inter-war period so that total entries, premiums and sums insured scarcely moved upwards. Post the management reconstruction in the 1950's the composition of the Club changed dramatically and with it the need for more comprehensive and expensive re-insurance.

The cover purchased edged up progressively in the 1950's and early 1960's and it was considered prudent in 1960 to buy a layer of £500,000 excess of £500,000, i.e. cover up to £1,000,000. This psychological barrier of £1,000,000 was soon to be breached however but not before much soul-searching debate in the Board about exactly where the British Marine was going. Eventually the re-insurance

ERKABURG (Class 1, Briese Schiffahrts and Co., Leer, Germany) is typical of a flexible breed of 2,000 d.w.t. Sea-Rhine trader fitted for containers and strengthened for heavy lifts.

treaty for the 1962/63 year was fixed for Class 2 containing the condition: "Amount insured, two million pounds, excess of a million pounds." Cover thereby ran up to £3,000,000. British Marine had broken through to become a truly international insurer. This final layer cost only £250!

British Marine's expertise as the insurer of the smaller more specialised type of ship became widely recognised by the other London P.&.I. clubs. For around a decade until 1964 the United Kingdom Club, one of the world's largest, was re-insured by British Marine for a section of its entered fleet to the mutual satisfaction of both. Certainly the smaller club made a modest underwriting profit from the exercise and when the arrangement was concluded the French fishing vessels of the mutuals La Mer and La Patrimoine were taken on risk, again profitably. In 1960 an approach was made by the Steamship Mutual who proposed that British Marine re-insure a fleet of some three hundred British, Irish, Dutch and German coasters for them by taking a 75% line. Unfortunately the proposal foundered on the complexities of management costs and the re-insurance treaties for unlimited liability within the pooling system of the International Group. There were no hard feelings as a few years later British Marine was re-insuring a fleet of Dutch coasters with the Steamship.

E.R. Evans and Company had been brokers as well as the Association's managers and prior to 1953 had placed its re-insurance at Lloyd's. After the demise of the management contract with E.R. Evans and Company and the winding up of that company, British Marine turned to C. Rowbotham and Sons for its increasingly complex re-insurance needs. This relationship proved to be satisfactory and lasted until the retiral of the Rowbotham principal when Bland Payne were engaged, in 1975, as advisors on market placings for both P.&.I. and

*Boston Deep Sea Fishery's CONINGSBY, built in 1927, contrasts significantly with the same
company's stern trawler of half a century later.*

*BOSTON HALIFAX
was built in 1975 and is
a typical example of the
stern trawler of that time
that came into British
Marine after the
amalgamation with the
United Kingdom
Trawlers Mutual.*

the developing Hull class.

In principle British Marine was using the well tried re-insurance techniques common to many clubs such as the pooling arrangement of the International Group. Whereas a Group club absorbed a proportion of a claim and passed the rest on to the other clubs in the pool who would then bring in the proprietary re-insurers if the pools limit was exceeded, British Marine would absorb or retain a specific amount of a claim and then progressively bring in a number of different re-insurers at different levels until the full cost of the claim had been met. Of the premium collected from the member the Association retained enough cash to

The 1963 PUTFORD ACHATES of Putford Enterprises Ltd. of Lowestoft (England).

meet its likely commitments (it invested this money until it was needed to meet claims) and then paid the re-insurance premiums negotiated annually with the underwriters. If it got these calculations correct the members were fully insured and no supplementary call was ever required.

From mid-1970's onwards British Marine was developing the strength of its two main classes, Hull and P.&.I., and as they expanded and altered in their composition the structure of the re-insurance programmes had to change accordingly. It was also a time of relatively high inflation and as the quantum of claims rose the levels at which re-insurances were brought into effect to protect the membership against the exceptional calls needed to be adjusted upwards. Excess of loss layers which had been effective at one time were overtaken by these trends and became inadequate and even uninsurable with the re-insurance underwriters.

It would be tedious in the extreme to attempt to record the twists and turns of

Crescent Shipping's LUMINENCE (built 1977, 1596 g.r.t.), was entered for both Hull and P.&I. cover. She specialised in cable laying, as the structure of her bow demonstrates, and is here seen after working in the Cook Strait, New Zealand. (Wellington Evening Post, New Zealand)

the annual restructuring of re-insurance treaties over the years but it is worth stressing that the outcome of these negotiations was of fundamental importance to the protection of the members and the successful growth of the Club. In this, for more than a decade now, the Board and Management have worked closely with Sedgwick Marine as British Marine's brokers. The relationship was interactive as the brokers contributed constructively on many occasions to the reshaping of the programmes and, once they were agreed, negotiated the cost of purchasing the protection in the re-insurance markets.

The well-publicised difficulties of Lloyd's in recent years and the consequent reduction in the ability of the London Market to offer as much re-insurance as it once did, has caused British Marine to look to European, Bermudan and American re-insurers for the cover its members need. The objective set by the Board, and ably carried out by Management, has been to avoid having to ask for supplementary calls in any class. The re-insurance programmes are structured specifically with that in mind and the "new" insurers have come on board to support that aim. Class 1 now operates under a quota share system, i.e. the re-insurer accepts British Marine's underwriting standards and accepts a fixed percentage of the risk for the same percentage of the premium. Added protection is obtained by way of excess of loss cover. Class 2 has the more familiar structure of the Association carrying a retention, i.e. the first layer of any claim with excess of loss layers providing cover of hundreds of millions of pounds sterling should such sums ever become necessary.

In the past a member of the British Marine paid an initial call and then a supplementary which was adjusted for his own claims experience. (As we have seen this worked quite well when essentially everyone's risks were the same. But it failed to serve members' interests when the spread of membership, and therefore risk, became much wider.) In this way the member spread his own risks. Today through the mechanisms of individual rating and re-insurance every member contributes to the spreading of all risks. The philosophy is still mutual but the application is quite different.

British Marine has come a long way from the days when a £6,000 hull risk was split between three clubs and even from the more recent time when it was thought adequate to take another layer of protection in excess of a million pounds.

John De L. Lewis, General Manager of British Marine from 1974 until 1993.

Claim: "What is in a Name?

British Marine is often asked to give financial guarantees to port or customs authorities to secure the release of a ship after an incident, e.g. damage to a quay in a port where the vessel is unknown or an infrequent caller. Some of the reasons given for requiring security can be unusual.

At first sight the case of the DIEKSEE aroused some suspicion. She arrived at Cherbourg (France) in 1979 having been seen by the French Navy to be lying in Barfleur Bay with a new name, REEFER TRADER, being painted on her bows. She was loaded with arms and ammunition for which she had no cargo manifests and was about to load more munitions for South Africa. All of the ship's papers were in the name DIEKSEE. She was arrested by the French customs who forcibly discharged the whole cargo and examined it package by package. Further, they refused to release the ship until a large guarantee in French francs was forthcoming.

A clear case of illegal gun-running with which British Marine should not become involved? Well, not quite. The owners were specialised carriers of arms and munitions and had transported such cargoes literally all over the world and had no previous difficulties of the kind experienced in Cherbourg. The receivers of the South African part of the cargo were hyper-sensitive to the possibility of the shipments being observed by 'outside' interests and had requested the owners to change the name of the ship for security reasons. This request was passed to the master who thought that he would save time by repainting the bows while he awaited his berth in Cherbourg. When the owners representative arrived with documentation in the name of REEFER TRADER the ship had been arrested.

International pressure from the consignee Governments eventually secured the release of the cargo. (The South African rockets were delivered by another ship and another route.) But the French customs, who had incurred hefty stevedoring costs, stuck to their demand for the large guarantee. It was pointed out to them that an appropriate fine for the breach in port regulations involving the wrong ship's papers and not following the advised procedures for loading explosives was one hundredth of the sum being demanded. British Marine allowed the claim for a sum equivalent to the fine and for legal costs. After the detention of the ship for eight months the owner struck a bargain with the Customs and she sailed.

THE SHETLAND CONNECTION. Built in 1994 for J.P. Duncan of the Shetland Isles the ALTAIRE (2274 g.r.t.) is a splendid example of the latest thinking in the design of deep sea fishing vessels. At one time one of the most valuable single hulls entered in British Marine she belongs to a group of Shetland based m.f.v.'s that make up one of the Association's most valued connections. Before 1978 there was no towage tradition in the Shetlands to match their centuries old fishing expertise, but when the Sullom Voe oil terminal came on stream and Shetland Towage Ltd. began operations, the innate ship-handling expertise of the Islanders, when applied in tugs like STANECHAKKER (entered in Class 1 and 2), soon helped make it a port with an enviable safety record.

Expansion and Absorption

The formation of new companies and the takeover of others are not activities that are normally associated with the somewhat sedate world of mutual marine insurance. Nevertheless British Marine must plead guilty to having indulged in both. At least the takeovers were amicable affairs as is appropriate for what is in essence a descendent of the old 18th century friendly societies.

At much the same time as British Marine was re-opening Class 1 a group of British shipowners were setting up another hull club in response to steeply rising rates in the proprietary market. Named the Short Sea Mutual Insurance Association Ltd (S.S.M.), to reflect the trading interests of the members, it began underwriting in March 1971. It was managed by a company in which S.S.M. had a 50% shareholding and was therefore partly independent of the membership.

It would appear that S.S.M. struggled from the start. A year after opening for business it had attracted only sixty vessels, mostly from the fleets of its founding committee. It was to reach a peak membership of fifty owners in 1975/76 but this declined quite rapidly when its difficulties became widely known. It was considered prudent to buy re-insurance for total loss, etc, but S.S.M. found that it was very expensive relative to its small initial entry. British Marine, of course, had a similar experience in re-starting its Class 1. This problem was compounded when underwriting losses were incurred, the solvency of some of its re-insurers became doubtful and administrative problems arose in the new company. By the 1976/77 policy year the number of entered ships had fallen to the start-up level.

An appeal for help was made to British Marine. Tradition has it that the discussions between the two Managements took place in a hostelry in the City of London but this must be doubted as it would have been unusual then, as it would be today, for important negotiations to take place in such informal surroundings. The outcome was that British Marine re-insured S.S.M. from August 1977 onwards and with the agreement of its Board took over the underwriting in February 1979 when S.S.M. formally ceased to do so on its own account. G. W. Thomas, Chairman of S.S.M., joined the Board of British Marine and successfully acted as liaison between the two clubs. The conflict of interest was more apparent than real and he dealt with the situation in a thoroughly professional manner. (He was to remain as a director for fourteen years and latterly became the Association's Vice-Chairman.) The possibility of a merger of the two mutuals was actively considered during 1980 but it was decided that S.S.M. would go into run-off and it was eventually put into voluntary liquidation in 1983. The small surplus that remained was returned to those that had been members. As a result of taking over the underwriting British Marine was able to offer renewal terms directly to some valuable new accounts like those of Coe Metcalf, ARC Marine and Lapthorn who have remained members to this day. It was a painless takeover. No assets were purchased, if those liquid ones that were exchanged in that first discussion in the licensed premises are discounted. British Marine received a handsome return on its investment.

It was as well that the Management, which was about to become so deeply involved with S.S.M., had just completed another far-reaching initiative. The Association had decided to go offshore to Bermuda in 1976. In contrast to the larger London based P.&.I. clubs British Marine had been slow to adopt such a policy.

The spur to this activity in the 1970's was the accumulation of funds in the Association from the growing Class 2 and the re-established Hull class. The monies retained from premiums to pay claims up to the levels at which the re-insured layers became active was placed in interest-bearing deposits for the benefit of the members until it was needed. What is more investments were held in the various currencies in which premiums were paid (this allowed claims to be met without the risk of exchange losses) and advice on international money markets was needed. Counsel was taken on how best to administer this developing situation and the advice was to form a Bermudan subsidiary company for the purpose of investing the funds and to act as a re-insurance vehicle. A subsidiary company would have administration expenses so that the benefits from its investments had to exceed these basic establishment costs. This was a function of size and the assets of British Marine had grown in 1976 to the point where going offshore made sense.

British Marine (Bermuda) Ltd was registered in February 1976 and the firm of Conyers, Dill and Pearman were appointed as its managers. The Board consisted of both U.K. and Bermudan representatives and

SHELL ROADBUILDER. (World Ship Photo Library)

Claim: "Bravery and Skill Recognised"
Not all payments made by the Association have been for insured risks. The mv WIDDALE H, (built 1954, 274 g.r.t.), carrying 340 tons of motor spirit ran aground in Swansea Bay (Wales) and remained fast on a falling tide. Another vessel, REGENT JANE, stood by but because of her draft was unable to approach and contacted the passing SHELL ROADBUILDER for help. The latter prepared to tow the stranded ship but could not use rocket apparatus to shoot a line because of the danger of explosion. Captain Ryder of the SHELL ROADBUILDER decided he had to go alongside the WIDDALE H which was by then lifting and pounding in the breaking seas. Seven times Ryder made an approach and on the four occasions that he got a line aboard it parted. Having used all his own cable he borrowed one from the REGENT JANE. In complete darkness his last effort was made within 30 feet of the cliffs but when the attachment was made and the tow commenced the WIDDALE H dropped into a trough and the bollards of the SHELL ROAD-BUILDER were pulled from her deck. Petrol fumes from the pounding vessel precluded any further attempts. In all Ryder stood by for eleven hours. The crew of the WIDDALE H waded ashore at low tide and the ship herself became a total wreck. A constructive total loss claim was paid.
   In view of their "magnificent seamanship" the Directors of the British Marine made a special award to the master and crew of the SHELL ROADBUILDER. The Silver Medal of the Royal Society of Arts for a deed of outstanding professional merit by a member of the British Merchant Navy was awarded to Captain Ryder.

CARHELMAR, a beam trawler, seen here with her beams out, was built in Holland in 1989 for J.H. Lovell, and has been a Hull and Machinery member since.

a re-insurance agreement was signed and sealed by the parent and new company. The benefits to the members came from investment yields that were apportioned among the Classes and had the general effect of reducing the impact of increases in premiums. The growth of the assets of the Association are to be seen in Appendix IV and there is no doubt that the Bermudan company contributed significantly to the rate of increase. The links with Bermuda have grown as not only do Bermudan companies participate in the Association's re-insurance programmes but the Bermudan Government's passenger ferries and tugs are entered in Class 1.

Typical of the passenger ferries that ply in the Great Sound in Bermuda, CANIMA, like the harbour tugs owned by the Government of Bermuda, is insured for Hull and Machinery by British Marine.

Of equal importance in the growth of British Marine was another event which followed hard on the heels of the S.S.M. 'acquisition'. From the very earliest days British Marine had insured fishing vessels, as a specialised activity within its mainstream business, and in 1964 had re-insured two French fishing mutuals. It was not to be until the 1980's that this type of ship became significant in numerical terms in the Association. The British fishing mutuals had developed, like many others, on a strongly localised basis. Round the coast where there were established fishing fleets the instinct to insure mutually was a natural consequence. The Humber ports on England's East coast had a long fishing tradition and it is not surprising that Hull became the base for an organisation that came to be important for fishermen throughout the country for the provision of their hull and indemnity cover, the United Kingdom Trawlers Mutual (U.K.T.M.). It was this Association that was to provide British Marine with an injection of new members.

Dredging International, based in Zwijdrecht, Belgium, enters its craft in Class 1 of the Association. BIG BOSS is a backhoe dredger that can dig to a depth of 24 metres.

In the 1970's and 1980's the fishing industry was undergoing a period of rapid change to a large extent due to the impact of the United Kingdom's membership of the European Economic Community and to technical changes in the industry itself. Stocks of fish were declining as were the number of fishing vessels as a consequence. Replacement tonnage was becoming more sophisticated and expensive in the effort to catch the remaining fish. In short, the U.K.T.M. could see that its entries would be reduced in the long term and that if the burden of its organisation, which had grown to service its members, fell on decreasing numbers it would become uncompetitive. Rather than wait until that happened the U.K.T.M. decided to look for a partner and not unnaturally its eye fell on a

VLAANDEREN I is a split trailing suction dredger of Decleodt and Fils.

recently rejuvenated mutual well known on the Humber for its book of specialised small ships, the British Marine Mutual.

Discussions between the two clubs began in 1981 and by the end of that year they were co-operating on the entry and re-insurance of some larger fishing boats than had been entered up to that time. A brief flirtation took place between the two and the Shipowners Mutual Protection and Indemnity Association but the proposition that a ménage à trois be established came to nothing. This was followed by somewhat protracted negotiations about a merger and real issues arose. Department of Trade approval was needed for an amalgamation or takeover. Unlike the case of the S.S.M., there was no rescue operation needed for the smaller club. (Approximately three hundred and sixty vessels were in the U.K.T.M. at this time and British Marine had a hundred more in the Hull class and seventeen hundred entered for P.&.I.) Understandably they were anxious to preserve the interests of their members. The indemnity cover offered by the U.K.T.M. was unique to them and these matters affected both the primary and re-insurance needs of the possible merged organisation. With considerable input from the re-insurance brokers Sedgwick Marine, these difficulties were resolved and from 20th February 1983 British Marine began to re-insure the business of the U.K.T.M. in all its aspects.

The intention was that from the beginning of the 1984 insurance year U.K.T.M. would cease to underwrite risks in its own right and would be merged with the British Marine. The final discussions on the merger and the obtaining of Department of Trade approval for it overran the 20th February renewal date and the temporary re-insurance arrangement had to be extended. Most of the Hull-based staff of the fishing mutual were retained to administer the fishing book and to supervise the run-off of the extant claims. The U.K.T.M. office at Hull was kept open for this purpose. The Chairman of the U.K.T.M., G.A. Marr, joined the Board of the new combined Association which began life slightly later than planned, on 31st October 1984.

In financial terms this was an important step as the underlying strength of the merged Association became materially greater. The geographic spread of the membership became much wider taking in important fishing fleets from the Shetland Islands off the North of Scotland to the Pacific Coast of North America. There can be no doubt that this broad base has enabled the British Marine to grow in recent years.

Claim: "Shifting Sands"
After a three month voyage from Newcastle (Australia) to Guayaquil (Ecuador) the ship HILSTON (built 1885, 2087 g.r.t.) anchored off the island of Puna in the approaches to Guayaquil in February 1913. The master's report of the next event of any note reads:

```
"Struck heavily on the bar and took a heavy list to port shortly after an
earthquake shook the vessel."
```

The ship was towed to drydock for repairs after being lightened by about a thousand tons of cargo.

"The Only London Club"

British Marine has always been a London Club. Indeed it has always been a City of London Club having not once in its history strayed far from the Square Mile. Edward R. Evans' first office was in New London Street in 1876 and his second in Philpot Lane (off Fenchurch Street) in 1885. It was three years before he moved again and then only to Lime Street at the corner of Leadenhall Market. We don't know exactly why he moved but we can speculate that the growth of the Association necessitated more staff and larger premises. The quill pen atmosphere of the establishment no doubt played its part in convincing the 1950 committee that it was time for change in management style and structure. The next change of location did not come until 1960. Then the Association relocated to Colchester House adjoining Trinity House and a few yards from the present office at Walsingham House in Seething Lane where it has been since 1978. Soaring property costs in London in the 1980's prompted consideration of moving to Hull, where an office was still maintained, but property bust followed property boom and it was found to be less expensive to rationalise the business into one location in London and to keep the advantage of proximity to brokers and re-insurers. A London Club it remains. There may have been a reluctance to move physically but, more importantly, the Association has moved a great distance commercially.

In the twenty years since Anthony Brown's brief history of British Marine was published much has changed and the rate of change has been accelerating. Then the Hull class was an infant taking its first tottering steps. It was not thought likely to overtake its older sibling which was striding out anew after having overcome earlier doubts about its own survival. These twenty years have seen a thirty-fold growth in premium income and a major upward revision of the limits of insurance that the Association offers. Certainly there has been inflation in that period but the larger income of the mid-1990's is more properly attributable to a larger entry from a wider geographic area of a more diverse fleet of ships of higher capital value.

Todays British Marine is an organisation of some forty skilled staff underwriting around four and a half thousand vessels. Approximately one thousand seven hundred claims worth £32 million are settled annually. Claims in Class 1 are usually paid within a year to eighteen months of notification but because of the complexity of some of the issues Class 2 claims can take twice as long to settle. As a result it is not unusual to find that well over three thousand claims are being processed at any one time with the sum involved of the order of £60 million. Little wonder there is a virtually constant investment in computer technology to deal with this.

From 1953 onwards British Marine was determined to widen the base of its membership beyond the geographic limit implied in its name. It attracted good northern European shipmanagers in the first instance, but that only began a trend

Richard D. Leslie, appointed General Manager in 1993.

that was to lead to the build up of world-wide entries in both of the main classes. Four thousand five hundred ships were entered in 1996 and this is six times the number of twenty years ago.

The shipowner of 1996 needs no reminder of the trend in new-building costs over this period. Today he owns fewer but larger and more sophisticated vessels. They are built for more specialised trades and have greater capital investment in automation. Does this account for the fact that what cost him a dollar, guilder, kroner, mark or pound in 1975 now costs ten times as much? If it does it also helps explain why British Marine has had to revise upwards its limits in response and accounts for some part of the premium growth.

Class 1 is now the dominant of the two, the premiums being approximately four times that of the P.&.I. class. It has nevertheless shown an inherent strength of its own although its rate of growth has been slower. Premiums from the Hull class began to overtake those of Class 2 in the mid-1980's (the merger with U.K.T.M. helped in this) and have grown dramatically since 1992. Growth per se in an insurance company is no guarantee of success. If premium growth is achieved without stringent underwriting standards it can only lead to disaster. It may be tempting to risk expansion at the cost of the loss ratio or to retain business in soft markets by offering unjustified renewal terms but at the end of the day somebody

O.I.L.Ltd. became Class 1 members in 1994, as did their fellow subsidiary of Ocean Group plc, Cory Ship Towage Ltd. Their OIL PROVIDER, 1590 g.r.t., purchased by them in 1994, operates in South East Asia as an anchor handling tug supply vessel. (D.G.S. Ltd.)

Claim: "Man Bites Dog"
Countless claims have been submitted over the years for ships hitting quays, jetties, bridges and lock gates. Indeed there is one continental port, which is assiduous in pursuing ships for the slightest damage to its facilities, that British Marine has almost completely rebuilt. In the case of the barque AMULREE (built 1892, 1445 g.r.t.) the claims book reports:

    "At Liverpool the quay wall collapsed outward and struck the ship damaging two
    plates and breaking all moorings."

The ship was repaired if not completely rebuilt by the port authority.

has to pay. In a mutual organisation that somebody is the member. If, on the other hand, you have decided against relying on the escape route of the supplementary call then you don't sail down the channel of buying growth. British Marine has not voyaged in that direction.

Many factors have contributed to this expansion but what cannot be discounted is the Association's unique position in the market place as the only London club that offers:

- a mutual basis for hull and machinery cover.

- mutual P.&.I. insurance outside the International Group.

- the advantages of direct control of the Club's management.

Many shipowners have come to appreciate that the distinction between the Association and the proprietary hull insurers, and the independence from the

Sosema's offshore supply vessel RED LARK discharging at an offshore installation, is entered in the Hull and Machinery class. (Sosema is the acronym for Societie De Service Maritime of Switzerland.)

consortium that is the International Group of P.&.I. Clubs, offers them genuine choice in their decision making. Historically this autonomy has been valued by the members and their representatives on their Board and is one of the principles that has guided British Marine throughout its existence. And as it grows in strength of numbers of members and assets no doubt it will continue to do so.

The various, and to date unconsummated, approaches to the British Marine, recorded elsewhere in this history, have been because of the attractions of the hull book. Those, no matter how large they are, who operate only in the single market of P.&.I. have wished to strengthen themselves by widening their appeal. The allure of the premium income of the third largest hull book in London is considerable. The attraction to British Marine of improving the competitiveness of its P.&.I. through the economies of scale offered by joining a larger grouping are more apparent than real. The possibility of lower rates for some levels of re-

Rimorchiatori Riuniti's firefighting azimuthal tractor tugs (No. 80 is GERMANIA, No. 81 SVEZIA and No. 83 FRANCIA) are seen here off their home port of Genoa (Italy). These 3,000 B.H.P. vessels were built in 1987/8.

insurance exists but the opportunity to achieve the same position by growth would be precluded. The potential benefits on offer have not been thought to compensate for the loss of independence that was entailed or for the sacrifice of a philosophy which was based on management for the shipowner by the shipowner.

The non-profit making concept is another which is widely appreciated by the ever cost conscious shipowner and as long as this is allied to an effective but sympathetic philosophy towards claim settlement then it will be perceived that value for money is being given. Many members have taken the long view and valued predictability more than year on year variations in initial call indications. Experience has often shown that the cheapest insurance on offer at the beginning of a year can turn into something a good deal less attractive after the cost of the subsequent supplementaries is taken into account.

In the last twenty years thirty men (no women as yet) have served the British Marine as Directors. Of these three have been Chairmen. Coincidentally all three, C. Crosthwaite, A.B. Wilbraham and L.J. Paterson, have been tugowners although both the North British Maritime and Clyde Shipping groups had wider interests. Some shipping men regard the towage operator with some suspicion and may see in this another example of a tugowners' plot to exercise undue

The sheer size of the modern multi-hull high speed ferry is illustrated here by the sight of the familiar public transport bus nestling comfortably beneath the hull of Condor Shipping Ltd's CONDOR 9.

influence. But the tug exemplifies the British Marine entries; the relatively small, expensive, sophisticated and specialised ship and in that way are as representative as any of the membership. Endorsed in their position by their fellow directors rather than appointed in apostolic succession these three have interacted with the professional insurance managers and staff to serve the day-to day business of shipping and move the Association forward.

Cecil Crosthwaite may be considered to have had the most exciting time having overseen the rebirth of Class 1 and the formation of the Bermudan subsidiary.

The OIL BONNY was built in the U.K. in 1993 and is a 274 g.r.t harbour tug currently working in Nigeria. (Hal Mullin)

Tony Wilbraham was the leading figure in the amalgamations with the Short Sea Mutual and the United Kingdom Trawlers Mutual. Len Paterson, who was Wilbraham's Vice-Chairman, has presided over a period of consolidation, growth and increasing internationalism. Crosthwaite, Wilbraham and Paterson were as different from each other as was Lewis from Leslie and yet over the two decades the permutation of any two from the five would seem to have met the challenges of the times. All were strong supporters of the mutual philosophy.

These thirty men have been involved with the operation of shipping as their main occupation. In a very real sense they are typical of the membership. As shipowners/operators they empathise with the member with the genuine claim. They can detect the spurious and the false and reject such claims in the interests of the other members. As businessmen in the international world of shipping they understand currency and investment dealings and tax regimes. Almost like no

The white fish trawler ANDROMEDA II, owned by A. Davidson, has been entered in the Association since 1995.

other commercial activity shipping forces its owners and managers to be cost effective in a truly international marketplace and in this respect the Directors consider value for money, either from premiums or management expenses, to be a sine qua non.

In other words the British Marine Mutual Insurance Association Ltd is about shipowner power - the only London club so uniquely constituted. The

Whilst well iced up herself and surrounded by the same crystallised water form HUBERT GAUCHER , Soconav Inc's 7687 g.r.t. tanker, manages to keep moving.

Claims: "Workmen's Compensation"
The following claim illustrates an interesting piece of British social history. The principle behind the workmen's compensation law was that if an employee sustained an injury or was killed at work compensation should be paid, according to a pre-determined scale, without the need to prove negligence on the part of the employer or a fellow workman. The first British Act was passed in 1897 but it was not until 1906 that the law applied to seamen. British Marine started to cover this liability in the P.&.I. class in 1907.

In 1908 the barque ISLE OF ERIN (built 1875, 941 g.r.t.) foundered and the master and a crewman were lost. The details of the compensation paid to the widows and of the claim on British Marine are given below.

```
Compensation for the loss of the captain    £300.00
Compensation for the loss of the crewman    £ 70.00
Recovery from re-insurance                   £286.75
               Net Claim on B.M.M.           £ 83.25
```

The contributing capital for Workmen's Compensation in Class 2 was £593,000 and the call for this claim was calculated thus:

$$£83.25 \times \frac{100}{593,000} = £0.014\% = 4 \text{ old pence.}$$

Payment for this claim was raised by asking members of the class to pay £0.014 for each £1 of capital they had insured for in the total of £593,000.

Taking into account the changed value of money the compensation paid for the master would be approximately £15,000 and that for the crewman £3,500 in today's terms.

STELLA PACIFIC of 4081 g.r.t. is owned by one of the Association's Swedish members, Lido Bulkers Ltd., and trades mostly in the Baltic.

shipowner's interests come first without any qualification whatsoever. Small though it may be in comparison with some in the P.&.I. market (and large in the hull reckoning) it points up some important lessons for those who would have greater control of their own destiny. More and more of those who wish to exercise that control will look to British Marine and to any other who adopts a similar philosophy as the medium for doing so. To achieve long term stable insurance for the shipowner British Marine is, of course, careful to keep re-insurers and regulatory authorities co-operative in all that it does. But by and large British Marine will have to stand or fall on its own decisions made in the interests of its members. This is what it has done in the past.

The past is here recorded and the knowledge and interpretation of it is essential to the future. To have lived to a thirtieth birthday, in human terms, is to be in one's prime with the reasonable expectation of seeing another thirty. After sixty birthdays, or two hundred and forty years of service, retiral might just be acceptable and appropriate. But with the constant renewal of the organism in the way we have seen since 1876 and in particular since 1976 retiral would seem to be a distant prospect indeed.

"Those who cannot remember the past are condemned to repeat it"

(George Santayana, 1863-1952.)

Claim: "A Philosophical Dispute"
In the case of ADAM SMITH v. VOLTAIRE, in 1916, the Directors decided to defend the P.&.I. member, the owner of the ADAM SMITH. This case was no doubt a repeat of these two bumping into each other 140 years previously when they had a candid and rational exchange of views on the wealth of their respective nations.

The FRESHFIELD (built 1954, 518 g.r.t),
owned by the Zillah Shipping Co. Ltd.

Claim: "A Limit to the Appeal of Guinness?"

In thick fog in the river Mersey (England), in 1961, THE LADY GWENDOLEN, proceeding up the river at 10 knots, collided with and sank the FRESHFIELD (a British Marine entry), which was lying at anchor. She was later raised but proved to be a constructive total loss. The case was to be a legal landmark in the case law of owners attempting to limit their liability.

THE LADY GWENDOLEN was owned by Arthur Guinness and Son (Dublin) Ltd., makers of the famous black stout, and their ship made regular trips from Ireland to England to deliver bulk quantities of their renowned product. At the time of the incident the Guinness ship was full of stout but at no time in the legal battles that followed was it ever inferred that the master of the ship was similarly pressed up.

The Guinness company admitted liability for the collision but sought to limit their liability to £23.65 per ton of their ship, a total of £21,135. Since the claim made by Zillah Shipping, the FRESHFIELD's owners, was of the order of £120,000 they were not at all happy with this.

The Guinness argument was based on the contention that the fault lay entirely with the master of their ship and that the incident occurred without their 'actual fault or privity', the usual form of words when seeking to avoid liability. This was resisted on the grounds that Guinness placed more importance on the master keeping to a schedule than to navigating safely. It was claimed that since the schedule was frequently met they should have known that their ship habitually travelled at 10 knots. It was argued that the master had not been properly instructed in the use of radar and specifically not told that he could not sail at 10 knots just because he had his radar switched on. The owners of THE LADY GWENDOLEN, because they could not claim to be unaware of these matters and could not prove that they had taken appropriate management action to correct them, were held to be at fault and not able to seek the protection of their right to limit their liability.

Despite the fact that the owners of THE LADY GWENDOLEN were not on the bridge at the time of the collision and the navigation of the ship was in the hands of her master and therefore outwith the direct control of the owners and that it was exceptional to question the fault or privity of an owner in respect of navigation, the experienced Admiralty Judge found that the loss occurred with their fault. Many shipowners found this to be a startling and worrying judgement that extended their management responsibilities beyond what they had previously considered to be their responsibility.

The Guinness company fought the decision all the way to the Court of Appeal and lost. They were also refused permission to appeal to the House Lords. It is not on record that their product lost any of its appeal as a result of the litigation.

Appendices

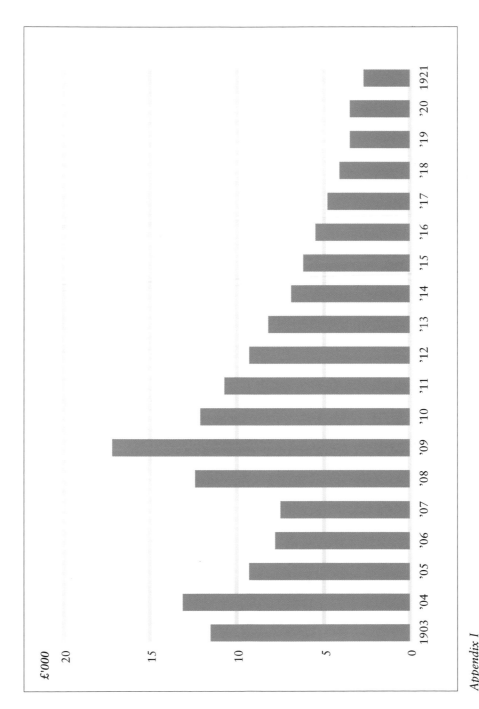

Appendix 1
Fall of Premium Income for Class 1, 1903 to 1921

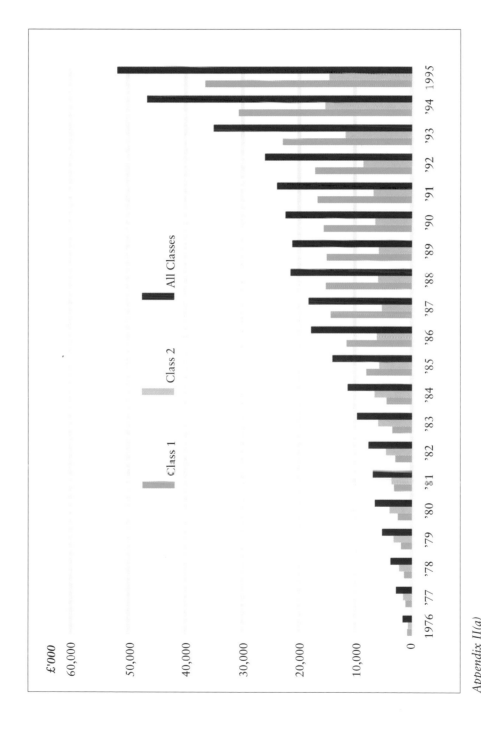

£'000

60,000

50,000

40,000

30,000

20,000

10,000

0

Class 1

Class 2

All Classes

1976 '77 '78 '79 '80 '81 '82 '83 '84 '85 '86 '87 '88 '89 '90 '91 '92 '93 '94 1995

Appendix II(a)
Growth of Premium Income for All Classes, 1976 to 1995

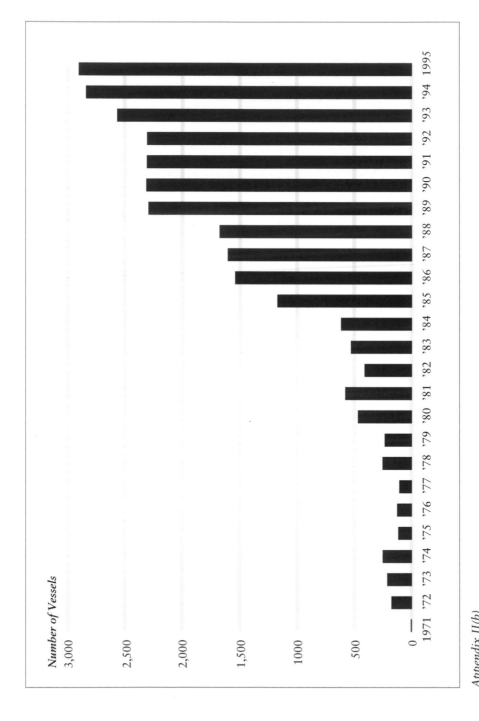

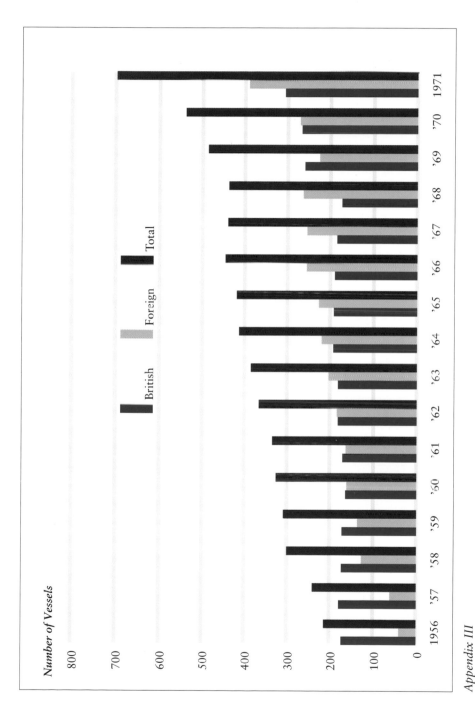

Number of Vessels

Appendix III
British and Non-British Entries, 1956 to 1971

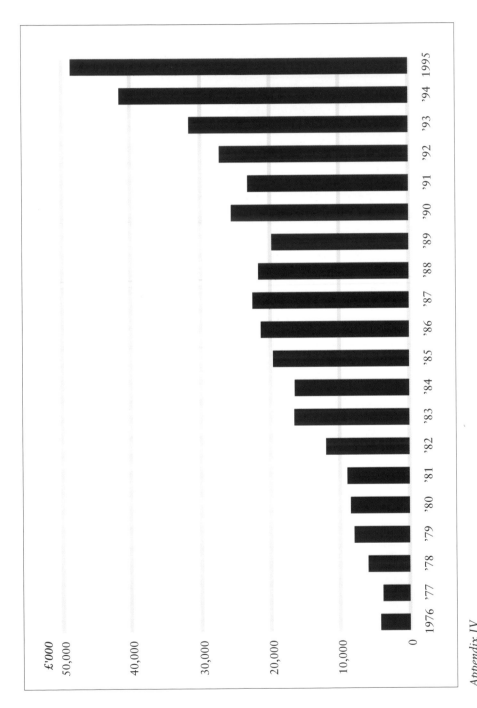

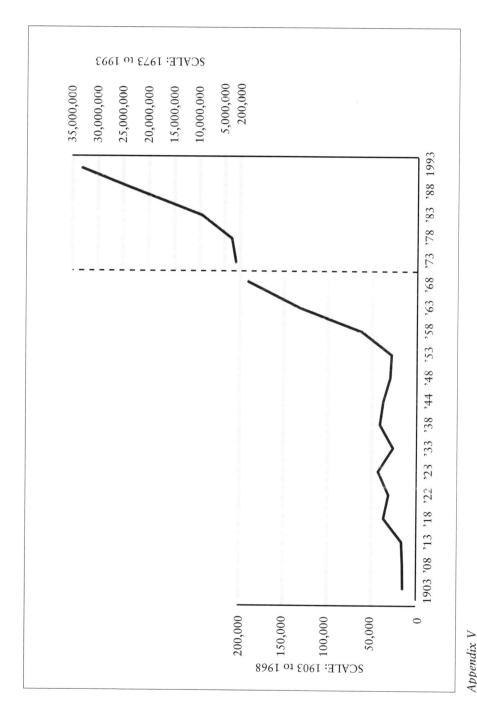

SCALE: 1973 to 1993

35,000,000
30,000,000
25,000,000
20,000,000
15,000,000
10,000,000
5,000,000
200,000

1903 '08 '13 '18 '22 '23 '33 '38 '44 '48 '53 '58 '63 '68 '73 '78 '83 '88 1993

200,000
150,000
100,000
50,000
0

SCALE: 1903 to 1968

Appendix V
Five Year Interval Call Income, 1903 to 1993

CHRONOLOGY

1866   E. R. Evans sets up in the management of marine mutual clubs for hull
(circa)   and freight insurance in London.

1876   Following the case of the Arthur Average Association the seven clubs that
          Evans managed are incorporated under the name of the British Marine
          Mutual Insurance Association Ltd.

1878   British Marine starts up a Protection Club.

1886   Indemnity cover is provided for the first time.

1894   British Marine is re-organised into four main classes - Hull, P.&.I.,
          Defence and Collision.

1907   Metropolitan Marine Mutual is set up. Workmens' Compensation Act
          cover is provided.

1917   British Marine joins the War Risks scheme.

1922   Class 1 (Hull) is put into run-off and is closed in 1925.

1939   British Marine offers War Risk cover from the beginning of World War 2.

1953   Re-organisation of the management of the Association proposed. The
          drive to attract continental European tonnage begins.

1955   The contract with E.R. Evans and Company is terminated and a new
          management structure is put in place. A General Manager is appointed.

1971   Class 1 for Hull and Machinery is re-opened.

1976   British Marine Mutual (Bermuda) Ltd is formed.

1977   British Marine re-insures the Short Sea Mutual and absorbs its
          membership in 1979.

1983   British Marine re-insures the United Kingdom Trawlers Mutual and
          merges with it in 1984.

1988   Class 4 (Collision) is merged with Class 1 (Hull).

1990   Class 5 (War Risks) is amalgamated with Class 1 (Hull).

Directors Since 1953

Name	Board service	Chairman	Vice-Chairman	Company
E.A. Gill	1909-1953			London & Rochester Trading Co. Ltd.
G.T. Gillie	1918-1959			G.T. Gillie & Blair Ltd.
W. Clint	1930-1955			John Kelly Ltd.
H. Brough	1933-1954			Zillah Shipping Co. Ltd.
T.E. Evans	1936-1953	1948-1953		T.E. Evans & Co. Ltd.
S. Moss	1937-1945			John Kelly Ltd.
C.B. Simpson	1937-1951			George Couper & Co. Ltd.
T.J. Tierney	1940-1951			Richard Hughes & Co. (Liverpool) Ltd.
T.F. Rice	1944-1954			James W. Cook & Son Ltd.
W.G.H. Stewart	1946-1948			
C.S. Rowbotham	1947-1974	1953-1971		C. Rowbotham & Sons (Management) Ltd.
C. Crosthwaite	1948-1978	1971-1978	1953-1971	Tees Towing Co. Ltd.
G.A. Tom	1948-1951			Geo. A. Tom & Co. Ltd.
G.C. Holt	1948-1962			John Kelly Ltd.
J. Todd	1951-1955			Hughes Holden Shipping Ltd.
E. Arnold	1952-1955			Harker (Coasters) Ltd.
M.O. Gill	1953-1974		1971-1973	London & Rochester Trading Co. Ltd.
S.F. Craggs	1953-1967			Hull Gates Shipping Co. Ltd.
W.P.M. Brough	1954-1959			Zillah Shipping Co. Ltd.
C.E.A. Fowler	1954-1964			Bulk Oil Steamship Co. Ltd.
P.S. MacCallum	1954-1970			Steel & Bennie Ltd.
M.E. Lyon	1955-1980			Lyon & Lyon Ltd.
E.W.P. King	1956-1968			John Kelly Ltd.
J.W. Dodd	1959-1962			Zillah Shipping Co. Ltd.
J.T. Gillie	1959-1989			Firth Shipping Co. Ltd.
D.C. Osborn	1962-1969			Osborn & Wallis Ltd.
P.S. Cross	1962-1968			W.A. Savage Ltd.
A.S. Tugwood	1965-1971			Cory Maritime Ltd.
A.B. Wilbraham	1967-1989	1979-1986	1978-1979	North British Maritime Group Ltd.
J.K. Wilson	1969-1978		1973-1978	John Kelly Ltd.
P. Dohle	1972-1974			Peter Dohle Schiffahrts KG.
P.A. Trace	1972-1978			Offshore Marine Ltd.
G.S.C. Clarabut	1974-1982		1979-1982	London & Rochester Trading Co. Ltd.
W. Devlin	1978-1991		1986-1990	John Kelly Ltd.
G.W. Thomas	1978-1992		1982-1984	Coe Metcalf Shipping Ltd.
A.F. Ford	1978-1980			Offshore Marine Ltd.
L.J. Paterson	1979-	1986-	1984-1986	Clyde Shipping Co. Ltd.
A. Greenwell	1979-1985			Tees Shipping Co. Ltd.
G.N. Elchlepp	1981-			Containerschiffsreederei H. W. Janssen Gbmh.
U.H. Heyenga	1981-		1993-1994	Thien & Heyenga Gbmh.
P.D.T. Roberts	1982-1985			London & Rochester Trading Co. Ltd.
G.A. Marr	1982-1988			J. Marr & Son, Ltd.
J. Bouwens	1984-1985			Gebr. Broere BV.
M. Heinimann	1985-1990			Union Trading Group PLC.
B.P.A. Cork	1985-1991			Star Offshore Services Ltd.
A.R. Winter	1985-1993		1990-1993	Hays Marine Services Ltd.

R.H. Cradock	1986-1995		Richard Irvin & Sons Ltd.
P.J. van Loef	1988-1989		Gebr. Broere BV.
F. Ollendorff	1989-1991		Mortenssen and Lange Ltd.
D. Robertson	1990-		L.H.D. Ltd.
D.M. Webb	1990-1993		Howard Smith (UK) Ltd.
C.L. Lister	1991-		Britannia Marine PLC.
P.H. Fagerlund	1992-		Knud I. Larsen Shipping Company.
B.A. Wheeler	1992-	1995-	ARC Marine Ltd.
T.C. Hart	1993-		Coe Metcalf Shipping Ltd.
J.K. McIntire	1994-		Tropical Shipping and Construction Co. Ltd.
P. Lynch	1995-		North Star Shipping (Aberdeen) Ltd.

Glossary

The following is a brief explanation, in non-technical terms, of some of the marine and marine insurance expressions used in the body of the book. Emphasis has been placed on producing a simple explanation rather than 'legal' accuracy.

Arbitration: the process of submitting a dispute to the judgement of an agreed person to avoid going to court.

Arrest: the detention of a ship because of an infringement of national or port rules or because of some other alleged or actual liability.

Ballast: material carried in a ship to improve its trim or stability when no cargo is loaded.

Bottom: a term sometimes used as an alternative to ship or vessel.

Broker: an expert in the law and practice of marine insurance who acts for the person insured to secure him the most advantageous insurance terms and is responsible to the insurer for the payment of the premium. Often termed as insurance broker to differentiate from brokers in other trades, i.e. shipbrokers, produce brokers, etc.

Brokerage: the commission, usually deducted from the gross premium by the broker for his services.

B.V.: Bureau Veritas, the French classification society, of which the top category is designated 3/3.LI.I. with a maltese cross.

Call: payments made to a mutual club by the members who enter their ships for insurance. The club adds up the costs of all claims and expenses and calls on the member to pay his proportion of the total.

Classification: the assessment of the standard of construction and maintenance of a ship by a recognised classification society, such as B.V. or Lloyd's Register of Shipping. If a vessel is not classified it may not be offered insurance cover or may be required to pay an additional premium.

Coastal Trade: a recognised set of geographic limits (mainland U.K., Channel Islands, Isle of Man and Ireland) within which a certain type of British ship was allowed to trade. Sometimes referred to as the Short Sea Trade or Home Trade.

Collision: actual contact with another ship. Collision is regarded as a peril of the sea and so damage caused to an insured vessel is recoverable.

Collision Clause: an important clause in all hull policies. It covers losses paid by the assured for damages to the other vessel, property on it, general average, salvage, etc. U.K. clauses limit the insurer's liability to three fourths of the sum assured.

C.T.L.: Constructive Total Loss, not an actual total loss of a ship but one which appears unavoidable or one where the expenses of recovery and repair are greater than the insured value of the vessel.

Cover: the guarantee given by the insurer to the insured to indemnify him in the event of a loss.

Deadweight: the carrying capacity of the vessel expressed in tons. Usually denoted by "dw" or "dwt".

Deductible: a stated amount of a claim which must be exceeded before the insurer will pay and then only the amount by which the deductible is exceeded.

Demurrage: compensation paid for the delay of a ship.

Deviation: the departure of a ship from the agreed, contracted or recognised course between two ports.

Excess of Loss: the protection against losing over a fixed amount. Cover is bought from a re-insurer to pay for claims above an agreed amount, the claims below that amount being paid for by the re-insured.

Free of Capture and Seizure: the clause in all marine insurance policies which excludes all the risks of war.

Flotsam: goods and materials lost from a sunken ship floating on the sea.

Freight: payment to the carrier for the transport of cargo.

Founder: the filling a of ship with water so that she sinks.

General Average: average is a partial loss. General average is a deliberate act, part of the ship or cargo being sacrificed to prevent the total loss of ship, cargo and freight. All of these three interests pay towards the cost of the partial loss.

Gross Tonnage: the total internal space of a vessel measured in units of one ton per 100 cubic feet. Often denoted as G.T. and formerly as g.r.t.

H. and M.: in the days of sailing ships stood for Hull and Materials but today stands for Hull and Machinery and is the type of insurance which covers damage to a ship's hull and her engines, etc. as distinct from P.&.I. insurance.

Indemnity: security of compensation against loss.

Jetsam: goods thrown overboard to lighten ship.

Jettison: to throw overboard.

Knot: the speed obtained when a vessel travels one nautical mile (6080 feet) in one hour.

Letter of Undertaking: a form of guarantee issued by an insurer promising to pay liabilities to avoid the arrest or delay of a ship.

Lloyd's: a corporation, based in London, that provides facilities for its underwriting members and syndicates to transact their business. Its members offer many other types of insurance as well as marine cover. The name dates from the time when underwriting began in the coffee house of a Mr. Edward Lloyd.

Lloyd's Register of Shipping: the U.K. ship classification society, founded in 1760. It has no direct connection with the Corporation of Lloyd's. The top category is denoted by 100A1 with a maltese cross.

Loadline: the mark on the side of a ship below which it must not sink when it is loaded.

Lien: a legal right to prevent someone taking possession of property, like a ship or cargo, until he has discharged his debt or other liability.

Line: the amount of liability accepted by an insurer. This can be the whole or only part of the liability and more than one insurer can participate.

Loss Ratio: the proportion that total claims is of the net premium income for any given period. When a shipowner's claims are more than the premiums paid, i.e. his loss ratio is more than 100%, he may be considered to have a poor claims record and would likely be asked for an increase in premiums.

Mutual Insurance: when a group of persons undertake to contribute to the losses of one of its members. The effect is that each insures the other. In marine insurance this occurs when shipowners form themselves into a mutual club.

n.r.t.: net registered tonnage, measured by subtracting the spaces for crew, stores and machinery from the gross registered tonnage. (N.T. formerly n.r.t.)

Particular Average: a partial loss other than general average.

P.&.I.: protection and indemnity, a form of insurance for the liability of shipowners to others or expenses unintentionally incurred in the running of a ship. These include, inter alia, liabilities for collision with fixed objects, for loss of life, fines, wreck removal, etc.

Quota Share: a system of re-insurance whereby the re-insured concedes an agreed proportion of his business to his re-insurers. Claims are re-imbursed in the same proportion.

Running Down Clause: another name for the collision clause.

Run-Off: the process of administering a claim or a group of claims to the point of final settlement.

Salvage: an award to a third party for services rendered to preserve a ship from perils of the sea.

Scuttle: to let water into a ship to sink it.

Sue and Labour: the shipowner may recover from his insurer any reasonable costs he has incurred to minimise the loss resulting from an incident. He may "sue labour and act in defence of his property" without prejudicing his rights under his insurance policy.

Syndicate: a group of underwriting members at Lloyd's in which each member accepts his proportion of liabilities accepted by the syndicate. Each underwriting member is known as a "name".

Warranted: promised by the insured.

War Risks Insurance: a type of insurance that covers those risks that the F.C & . S. clause excludes.